D1069383

CRISIS AND INTERVENTION

Lessons From the Financial
Meltdown and Recession

Edited by Glen Hodgson
Foreword by John Manley

The Conference Board of Canada • Ottawa, Ontario • 2010

The Conference Board of Canada
255 Smyth Road, Ottawa ON K1H 8M7 Canada
Inquiries 1-866-711-2262
conferenceboard.ca

Library and Archives Canada Cataloguing in Publication

Crisis and intervention : lessons from the financial meltdown and recession / edited by Glen Hodgson.

Includes bibliographical references.
Issued also in electronic format.
ISBN: 978-0-88763-954-8

1. Global Financial Crisis, 2008-2009. 2. Recessions--History--21st century. 3. Global Financial Crisis, 2008-2009--Government policy--Canada. 4. Recessions--Government policy--Canada. 5. Economic stabilization--International cooperation. 6. Global Financial Crisis, 2008-2009--Government policy. I. Hodgson, Glen David, 1955- II. Conference Board of Canada

HB3717 2008-2009 C75 2010   330.9'0511   C2010-907120-4

Printed and bound in Canada.   978-0-13-272418-0

Page design by Debbie Janes, The Conference Board of Canada.

Table of Contents

Foreword

by *The Honourable John Manley*

> Those who cannot remember the past
> are condemned to repeat it.
>
> —George Santayana

T his book is a concise and highly readable summation of the causes of the global financial crisis and the resulting lessons that need to be learned by both the public and private sectors.

The recent financial crisis taught us many things. But above all, I believe it offered a lesson in humility. I suspect that it will be many years before anyone ever again thinks of referring to Wall Street's high flyers as "Masters of the Universe." (That phrase is laughable today!) Or before anyone again ventures to speculate about "the end of the business cycle," as an article in *Foreign Affairs* did back in 1997. That widely quoted piece asserted that advances in technology and finance, along with globalization and smarter public policy, had reduced the volatility of economic activity in the industrialized world. Instead, it argued, "the waves of the business cycle may be becoming more like ripples." This book—*Crisis and Intervention*—would have been unnecessary if the turmoil that unfolded in our economies in 2007, 2008, and early 2009 had instead been merely a "global financial ripple."

As for the end of boom-and-bust, I'm certain that the 19th century Scottish journalist Charles Mackay would have recognized the recent expansion and collapse of the U.S. real estate market for what it was— yet another sad illustration of what he called "the madness of crowds." One of Mackay's famous observations was that men "think in herds [and] go mad in herds, while they only recover their senses slowly, and one by one."

So a little humility is in order. When things are going well, we have a distressing tendency to believe that somehow "this time is different" (a phrase that serves as the title to Ken Rogoff and Carmen Reinhart's stunning book describing eight centuries of financial catastrophes). We like to think of ourselves as quite a bit more intelligent and sophisticated than preceding generations.

As someone who has managed to acquire some experience in both government and the private sector, I am not among those who believe governments always have the best answers—that the wisdom of politicians and public officials automatically trumps the judgment of business owners and managers. This book makes clear that responsibility for the recent financial crisis is shared by the public and the private sectors.

The law of unintended consequences applies just as much to the making of public policy as it does to decisions in the financial sector and the broader business world.

Consider the unintended consequences of public policy that was designed to encourage home ownership in the United States but that ultimately led millions of people to buy more house than they could afford—and to regard real estate speculation as a "can't lose" proposition. Policies aimed at promoting the old-fashioned value of "home sweet home" instead bred a mentality of "flip this house" (to borrow the title of a popular reality TV series).

Similarly, was there ever a time in human history that the consequences of non-payment of a loan fell so gently upon borrower and lender alike? Non-recourse mortgages left borrowers—many having no equity invested to lose—free to drop off the keys at the bank and move on without fear of pursuit for the shortfall of a distress sale. Meanwhile, first-instance lenders had frequently bundled the mortgages into packages that were eagerly bought by others, and still others after them.

Could our ancestors who preached "neither a borrower nor a lender be" have ever imagined a sophisticated financial institution authorizing a "NINJA" (no income, no job, or assets) loan? It became, for a period of time, old fashioned to believe that one should be prudent about assuming debt. In the corporate sector, being underleveraged was an invitation to private equity to mount a takeover. (What a quaint concept "underleveraged" now seems!)

But if our goal is to build a more resilient global economy, we need to be careful not to look to tougher government regulation as a panacea. Well-intentioned but poorly thought-out policies might actually increase the problems of moral hazard and risk, or push risk aversion to such an extreme that the economy suffers. The key is to get the balance right. That means ensuring a fair, consistent regulatory environment with better international coordination and clearer rules of the game.

With respect to financial services, governments, regulators, and banks need to work together to improve the system in ways that will discourage excessive risk taking while facilitating international flows of capital and goods and promoting economic growth.

When things fall apart, when it becomes painfully obvious that trees cannot grow to the sky, there are always those who rush to embrace some grand scheme supposed to guarantee the turmoil will never happen again.

We saw that two years ago in some of the more simplistic calls to "reinvent capitalism," the implication being that only the heavy hand of government regulation can possibly save us from the excesses of the free market.

U.S. journalist and essayist H.L. Mencken once wrote, "Explanations exist; they have existed for all time; there is always a well-known solution to every human problem—neat, plausible, and wrong." This book is refreshingly free of simplistic, if elegant, solutions to the complex problems that led to our recent troubles. But it does highlight lessons learned that are sound and practical. Let's hope our decision-makers in the public and private sectors are listening.

Preface

by *Glen Hodgson*

Senior Vice-President and Chief Economist
The Conference Board of Canada • November 2010

In the autumn of 2009, the global economy was beginning to emerge from a truly exceptional event, the first synchronized global recession since the Second World War. The recession was caused by a financial crisis that was unprecedented in scale (although not unprecedented in type—there have been many other financial crises since the emergence of capitalism).

It struck me as an analyst and observer of the Canadian, North American, and global economies that some important lessons could be learned from what we had come through—the global financial crisis and recession of 2008–09. I invited (or perhaps more accurately, challenged) my colleagues—members of the excellent team of economists at The Conference Board of Canada—to work with me on a project that would define what those lessons are. Our aim was to share these observations and lessons with our client base in Canadian businesses, governments, academia, and elsewhere.

The lessons were initially published as a series of briefings, distributed electronically via The Conference Board of Canada's website. Having produced the soft-copy briefing series, the logical next step was to pull all of these briefings, along with a few other lessons, together into a single publication that could be made available to a wider readership. This book is the result.

I would like to thank the authors of the individual chapters for finding the time to respond to my challenge. No doubt other lessons can be drawn from the financial crisis and recession, but these are the key ones that we were able to identify from our various fields of expertise and experience.

Thanks as well to our dedicated reviewers: Anne Golden, Paul Darby, and Joe Haimowitz of The Conference Board of Canada; Sam Boutziouvis of the Canadian Council of Chief Executives; Christopher Ragan of McGill University; and Bruce Little. Thanks also to the Conference Board's Publishing department for the production of this book. Of course, any errors of fact or interpretation are those of the editor, the authors, and The Conference Board of Canada.

OVERVIEW

What Caused the 2008–09 Financial Crisis and Recession?

by *Christopher Beckman*

HIGHLIGHTS

- The collapse of Lehman Brothers in September 2008 was the catalyst for the frightening developments that followed—but it wasn't the only cause.
- There were many factors behind the global financial crisis that peaked in the fall of 2008—from the U.S. housing bubble to excessive financial innovation.
- The combination of a loss of confidence and a loss of access to credit for businesses and consumers created the conditions for recession in the U.S.—a recession that quickly spread around the globe.

On September 15, 2008, global financial services giant Lehman Brothers went under. In the two incredible weeks that followed, the Federal Reserve and the U.S. Treasury nationalized the country's two largest mortgage entities, Fannie Mae and Freddie Mac, and took over the world's largest insurance company, AIG. The government banned short selling in over 900 (mostly financial) stocks and promised to cough up $700 billion to purchase bad mortgage-related debt from the nation's banks. The dramatic moves by the U.S. government and the Fed were desperately needed. The bankruptcy of Lehman had sparked a panic in the commercial paper, credit-derivatives, and bank-funding markets that significantly worsened banks' balance sheets.

In the weeks and months that followed, global capital flows and trade flows spiralled downward, and a vicious cycle of credit withdrawal, halting of investment, weaker growth, and debt impairment took hold. The result was the first synchronized global recession since the late 1940s.

While the collapse of Lehman Brothers was the catalyst for the frightening developments that ensued, it certainly did not cause the financial crisis or subsequent recession. The failure of Lehman Brothers was merely a symptom of a larger problem that had been building for years.

A PERFECT STORM OF CONVERGING FACTORS

No single major issue lay behind the global financial crisis that peaked in the fall of 2008. Rather, it was a combination of elements that began converging in the summer of 2007 and continued to shake the world through the spring of 2009, including a global imbalance in savings and investment, a lack of savings (by U.S. households in particular), a surge in the U.S. subprime mortgage market, and new financial market innovations that were largely unregulated. Any one of these issues on its own would not have caused the severe global recession that began in late 2008. For instance, the excesses in the U.S. subprime market, without the presence of the other problems, would have undoubtedly hurt the American economy, but would not have come close to toppling the entire global financial system.

The story begins with the high-tech bust that resulted in a mild recession in the United States in 2001. This recession led the Fed to pursue an accommodative monetary policy and to reduce nominal interest rates sharply from the 6 per cent range that existed in 2000. Interest rates eventually reached a low of 1 per cent by the middle of 2003 and were still below 2.5 per cent at the end of 2004. Rates did not rise to a more normal level associated with a healthy economy until the spring of 2006, when they reached 5 per cent.

Not surprisingly, the low interest rate environment, together with strong U.S. economic growth and very low unemployment (the unemployment rate was below 5 per cent for much of 2006), led to a surge in home buying that naturally caused home prices to rise sharply. Between the end of 2002 and the summer of 2005, existing home sales increased by about 25 per cent. Similarly, median prices for existing homes increased by 37 per cent between the end of 2002 and the spring of 2006.

To push mortgage sales, many lenders approved loans for borrowers who weren't required to provide proof of employment or income, or who did not possess any assets.

It was not only low mortgage rates that led to a surge in housing markets in the mid-2000s. To entice potential homeowners—especially those with low incomes—into the market, mortgage lenders started offering "subprime" mortgages. These mortgages had a number of characteristics that appealed to low-income families, including low or zero down payments, long amortization periods, and low "teaser" interest rates that accelerated quickly after the initial year or two of the loan. Many of the mortgage lenders that cropped up during the early to mid-2000s were unregulated institutions. This was especially true in states such as California and West Virginia. To push mortgage sales, many lenders engaged in unscrupulous practices, such as approving loans to borrowers who weren't required to provide proof of employment or income, or who possessed no assets at all.

The terms "liar" loans and "ninja" (no income, no jobs, and no assets) loans became popular and will forever be linked to this period. Many of the individuals who took out these loans were seemingly unaware of the severe consequences of a decline in home prices. And when higher mortgage payments kicked in once the initial low interest rate grace period ended, interest rates on the subprime loans rose quickly, putting many mortgage holders at risk. The combined effects of falling house prices and rising mortgage rates meant many homeowners could no longer afford to pay or to re-finance their mortgages.

The U.S. government—under George W. Bush, but also under earlier administrations—had contributed to the formation of a housing bubble. Past administrations and Congress had made interest payments on prime-residence mortgages deductible from income taxes, which enticed consumers to buy larger and more expensive homes. The two government-backed mortgage lenders, Fannie Mae and Freddie Mac, were encouraged to make mortgage loans widely available to poorer households. Indeed, upon taking office, then-President Bush stated that one of his goals was to ensure that every American could eventually own a home.

Tax-deductible interest payments on prime-residence mortgages enticed consumers to buy more expensive homes.

While the housing market was taking off in the mid-2000s, some politicians in Washington were urging Congress to take steps to rein in lending practices in the subprime mortgage market, which was almost completely unregulated and already out of control. However, these were voices in the wilderness. Even the Fed chairman at the time, Alan Greenspan, contended that a bubble was not forming in U.S. housing markets and that financial markets continued to operate in an efficient manner.

Another development was the growing use of rising home prices as a means of financing additional consumer spending. Households used the incredible run-up in home prices to refinance their debt and get some extra cash that they used to buy more goods—boats, cottages, and new consumer electronics. The rise in household wealth due to the surge in home prices and in equity markets led American households to forgo personal savings. The savings rate actually fell into negative territory in 2007.

This mix of lax regulation, aggressive and dishonest lenders, naïve borrowers, and inappropriate policy responses by the Fed eventually led to a housing market meltdown beginning in late 2006. The collapse in housing markets then led to a severe recession in the U.S. economy. However, to explain why the subsequent recession eventually encompassed the entire world economy, we must examine other developments.

UNREGULATED FINANCIAL INNOVATION

The catalyst that spread the U.S. housing market meltdown to the rest of the world was the rapid innovation in global financial markets. The surge in U.S. housing markets coincided with the rise of new financial techniques, notably "securitization," a process that became quite common in financial markets in developed countries. Banks bundled up the mortgage loans on their books and sold them as securities in secondary markets (to hedge funds and other financial institutions). These loans became known as mortgage-backed securities (MBS). The bundling up and selling of mortgages to other institutions removed the risk from banks' balance sheets and enabled them to make new loans to other firms or individuals. Securitization was facilitated by the two government-sponsored mortgage-financing enterprises, Fannie Mae and Freddie Mac. They purchased mortgage loans from banks and bundled them into securities in order to increase mortgage funding sources and to make it easier for more Americans to buy their own homes.

The institutions that purchased the mortgage loan securities from banks often created collateralized debt obligations (CDOs) that contained pools of MBS and other loans with varying degrees of risk. The different levels of risk in a CDO, without adequate transparency, made it very difficult for potential buyers to understand exactly what they were buying. Rating agencies, such as Moody's and Standard & Poor's, often gave the CDOs AAA ratings even though there were potential conflicts of interest—the rating agencies were often paid by the institutions issuing the CDOs. A form of insurance for CDOs and other derivatives, called credit default swaps, also gained popularity. Trading in derivatives and credit default swaps was unregulated, so buyers of these complicated financial products took on an unknown—but often high—degree of risk.

The MBS were very attractive investments for buyers, since on the surface they offered much higher returns than lower-yielding government bonds. All over the world, banks, hedge funds, pension funds, and even municipalities snapped them up. As long as home prices in the United States were increasing, investors did not have to worry about households defaulting on their mortgages. But when home prices started to collapse in the second half of 2007, a growing number of homeowners were forced into foreclosure, and the securities backed by these mortgages started to default. The bad loans quickly began to erode the balance sheets of financial institutions that had purchased MBS.

> **MBS appeared to be attractive investments, since on the surface they offered much higher returns than government bonds.**

For the securitization process to work effectively, banks and other mortgage originators had to exercise appropriate due diligence on the mortgages that they originated. Without due diligence, the MBS market could run into serious problems—an inevitable development given the rise in the subprime loan market.

The first sign of trouble in global financial markets came in the summer of 2007, when the market for asset-backed commercial paper (ABCP) in the U.S. froze. Many companies depend on the short-term commercial paper market for their day-to-day financing requirements, but investors suddenly stopped buying ABCP due to concerns that it might be backed by mortgages in default. At the time, the Fed stepped in and provided liquidity to the market. This reassured markets. The LIBOR (London Interbank Offered Rate), the rate that banks charge each other for overnight lending, started to fall back down from the lofty heights it had reached amid the growing uncertainty in financial markets.

This intervention by the Fed, however, proved to be only a temporary respite. The wave of mortgage defaults grew and the balance sheets of certain financial institutions continued to deteriorate. In March 2008, the investment bank Bear Stearns collapsed under the weight of bad debt and was eventually sold to another investment bank—JPMorgan

Chase—at a price far below its earlier trading value. Equity markets sank on news of Bear Stearns' collapse, but soon recovered. However, financial markets quickly resumed their downward course, culminating in the events of September 2008.

FROM FINANCIAL CRISIS TO ECONOMIC RECESSION

As the global financial crisis gained momentum, it became virtually impossible for the real economy to avoid slipping into recession. Credit is a crucial input, both for households and for firms. Once credit dried up, business and consumer confidence plunged. Firms stopped investing and households slashed spending. The combination of a loss of confidence and a loss of credit created the conditions for recession in the U.S. that quickly spread around the globe.

Initially, many analysts felt that the developing world, in particular Latin America and Asia, could avoid recession because their banks had little exposure to MBS originating in the United States. As the downturn in the developed world gained steam in late fall 2008, however, the market for exports from Asia and elsewhere slumped badly. Similarly, declining commodity prices hurt parts of Latin America. China and India managed to blunt the impact of tumbling export demand from the developed world by engaging in massive monetary and fiscal stimulus efforts. China spent an estimated $2 trillion to keep its economy out of recession, of which more than $600 billion was new budgetary spending. China, India, and Australia (a major trading partner of China) were among the handful of countries that managed to escape the most negative fallout from the recession.

OIL PRICES ANOTHER FACTOR

In addition to the credit crisis, the price of oil played an important role in the recession. In early May 2007, world oil prices were around US$60 per barrel. By the end of the year, they had soared to almost

US$100 per barrel, and they eventually peaked at US$147 per barrel in July 2008. This represented a dramatic increase of 143 per cent over fifteen months! The surge in oil prices contributed to the decline in real consumer spending in 2008, especially in countries like the United States and Japan that rely heavily on oil imports. Households were forced to spend more on imported energy, leaving less to spend on other goods and services. It is difficult to quantify the precise impact of soaring energy prices in causing the recession because they occurred while the credit crisis was gathering momentum.

Would the global economy have collapsed under the weight of rising oil prices even if the credit crisis had not taken place? Possibly, but the world economy today is far less dependent on energy than it was in the early 1980s and 1990s, when high energy prices played a crucial role in sparking global downturns. Today, the services sector dominates economic activity in the developed economies. These economies no longer require as much energy to generate a dollar of gross domestic product as they did a few decades ago.

AFTERMATH OF GLOBAL RECESSION

The global recession ended in the second half of 2009, but the end of the recession did not mean a return to normality for world financial markets. While conditions improved markedly (as evidenced by more normal spreads between ordinary bonds and the virtually risk-free U.S. government bonds), they remained volatile, especially in the European Union. The steep recession led to a surge in government deficits and debt levels in developed countries around the globe, as revenues dropped and governments ramped up spending to mitigate the effects of the recession. The problem was especially acute in the so-called "PIIGS" countries—Portugal, Italy, Ireland, Greece, and Spain—which had been coping with huge deficits even before the global economy slipped into recession in 2008. The sheer magnitude of deficits in the PIIGS countries caused investors to balk at buying their government bonds, which forced the EU and the International Monetary Fund to put together a financial rescue package to provide emergency funding to EU members that could no longer tap into global financial markets to finance their deficits.

The difficulties were not confined to the PIIGS countries. Banks in Germany, France, the United Kingdom, and the United States were owed billions of dollars by debtors in these countries. Consequently, a failure of a Spanish or a Greek bank, or the inability of a government to meet its obligation on time, could quickly reverberate around the world—and potentially result in another 2008-style credit crunch. That is why banks in Europe were required to undergo stress tests to see if they were in a position to survive another global credit crisis. Other lingering signs of the 2008–09 credit crisis could be seen in the rock-bottom interest rates that remained in place in the EU, the U.S., and the U.K. long after the global recovery had begun. While low interest rates helped these countries avoid tumbling back into recession, they also added to the structural imbalances that will eventually have to be addressed.

The global economy is still feeling the effects of the financial crisis and the ensuing global recession. It could take many years—a decade even—before the global economy manages to completely shrug off the lingering effects of the events of 2008–09.

CONCLUSION

Several factors converged to create the global financial crisis and ensuing recession. American households let their savings slip and their debt levels soar in the low interest rate environment that followed the high-tech collapse in the early 2000s. This set the stage for the U.S. housing bubble as subprime mortgages were created in huge volumes, without the lenders exercising due diligence over the financially challenged mortgage holders. These mortgages were then bundled up and sold to other financial institutions around the world. The bundled securities were poorly understood and improperly valued. When the mortgages backing the securities began to default in large numbers, the stability of the global financial system was threatened. The ensuing plunge in confidence led to a huge drop in consumer and business spending, plummeting international trade, and a sharp global recession. The global economy is still dealing with the aftermath of the global recession that ended in the second half of 2009. The ongoing credit problems in the EU provide ample evidence of the damage that can occur when financial markets are thrown into the kind of turmoil that erupted in 2008.

LESSON 1

Sound Fiscal Policy Is Key to Keeping the Economy Afloat in Hard Times

by *Pedro Antunes, Sabrina Browarski,* and *Matthew Stewart*

HIGHLIGHTS

- An intelligently designed fiscal system is more than a tool for generating revenue that governments then spend—it plays a vital role in shaping a country's economic performance.
- Tax reform is only one part of the fiscal puzzle.
- Of all the fiscal stimulus measures, infrastructure spending has the largest impact on economic growth.
- Automatic stabilizers serve as a crucial economic buffer in times of economic downturn.

The eleven years leading up to the 2008–09 recession were boom years for Canada's federal government. Year in and year out, the government enjoyed stronger-than-expected revenue growth and large fiscal surpluses that were almost always larger than forecast. But even as it reaped the benefits, the federal government still found itself forced to make difficult choices. Everyone, it seemed, wanted a piece of the pie— and the pie was sliced up and handed out. The government cut personal and corporate taxes, delivered more generous transfers to the provinces and territories, and expanded federal programs. In general, though, the federal policy measures implemented over the decade leading up to the recession helped boost Canada's long-term economic growth prospects.

The provinces, too, reaped the benefits of rising revenue from their own sources and the generous growth in federal transfers. (Their capacity to implement productivity-enhancing policies, however, was weakened by their need to meet the ever-rising demand for health care.)

Then the recession struck. And early in 2009, federal and provincial governments responded with recession-fighting measures that included tax cuts, various tax credits, and a wide range of spending programs. How well have these measures worked?

THE RIGHT FISCAL SYSTEM CAN HELP GOVERNMENTS WITHSTAND RECESSION SHOCKS

An intelligently designed fiscal system is more than a tool for generating revenue that governments then spend—it plays a vital role in shaping a country's economic performance, productivity, international competitiveness, and sustainability for future generations. The way in which fiscal policies—taxation and spending—are framed determines the relative emphasis that businesses and citizens place on investment versus savings, and on work versus leisure. Moreover, a sound fiscal framework can play a vital role in supporting strong economic performance, not only in the good times, but also when recession hits. Ironically, the aftereffects of a recession provide a climate that is ripe for fiscal reform. So far, however, few countries have moved to seize the opportunity by implementing sound policies aimed at long-term fiscal sustainability.

> A sound fiscal framework can play a vital role in supporting a strong economic performance when a recession hits.

Economic research provides a valuable guide to the relative priority of various tax policies. In good economic times, such policies are aimed at boosting productivity, and in times of economic downturn, they are effective in inoculating an economy against recessionary shock or helping in its recovery. For example, Table 1 provides the results of recent research by Canada's Department of Finance, using what is called a general equilibrium model[1] of the economy to test the long-term impact of different tax cuts on households and the level of economic output.

Table 1
Impact of Various Tax Initiatives

Tax measure	Welfare gain ($) per dollar of lost present value in government revenue	Percentage change in steady state GDP for an ex ante 1 per cent of GDP reduction in government revenue
Increase in capital cost allowances on new capital	1.35	4.39
A cut in personal capital income taxes	1.30	3.36
A cut in sales taxes on capital goods	1.29	3.05
A cut in corporate income taxes	0.37	1.94
A cut in personal income taxes	0.32	1.29
A cut in payroll taxes	0.15	0.66
A cut in consumption taxes	0.13	0.19

Source: Maximilian Baylor and Louis Beauséjour, "Taxation and Economic Efficiency: Results From a Canadian CGE Model." Federal Department of Finance Working Paper 2004-10 (Ottawa: Department of Finance, 2004).

---

1 Researchers at Canada's Department of Finance developed a general equilibrium (GE) model to estimate the impact of various policy measures on the general welfare. The GE model offered a full accounting of how businesses, households, and government might be affected by various policy shocks, based on theoretical economic relationships. GE models are generally good at identifying the long-term equilibrium (i.e., when there is no excess demand or supply in any market) consequences of different policy measures. In Table 1, the welfare gain is defined as the ratio of the net gain to households versus the loss in the present value of government revenues due to the tax change. The second column displays the long-term impact on GDP relative to a 1 per cent of GDP change in the revenues from the tax. The amount of tax cut is calculated ex ante (previous to running the model) because government revenues are affected by the shock itself.

The research shows that targeted tax cuts that support investment by businesses and by individuals deliver, by far, the largest payback in terms of increased productivity, output, and improved general welfare. Furthermore, cuts to personal and corporate income taxes provide a boost to productivity and economic growth that is significantly larger than the boost provided by cuts to consumption taxes. The results of this research are consistent with the general body of economic literature and research on tax reform, both for Canada and for other nations.

But have policy-makers looked at the research and acted accordingly? The answer is generally "yes"—at least, for Canada. (Elsewhere, the actions have been less encouraging.) In the decade before the recession, Canadian tax reform was by and large positive, with productivity-enhancing initiatives implemented on many fronts. Canada entered the financial crisis in a very strong fiscal position relative to other developed nations. By the end of the 2007–08 fiscal year, Canadians were happily sitting atop a nearly $10-billion annual surplus—the eleventh federal fiscal surplus in as many years. Provincial fiscal balances had also strengthened considerably. Personal and corporate tax collections had been on the upswing, benefiting particularly from the commodities boom and growth in incomes for higher-income groups. The revenue growth more than supported rising federal program expenditures and transfer payments.

With ample fiscal manoeuvring room, the federal government was able to implement two successive 1 percentage point cuts to the federal goods and services tax—but at the price of reducing the potential federal fiscal surplus. This controversial move, which brought the GST rate from 7 to 5 per cent, reduced annual revenues by an estimated $10 billion to $12 billion. As shown in Table 1, economic theory suggests that cuts in consumption taxes have, by far, the smallest positive impact on GDP and on households. Thus, most economists agree that the government could have chosen more effective tax reduction measures at the same cost in forgone revenues.

That is not to say that other, more efficient, fiscal initiatives were ignored. Quite the contrary. At the federal level, the corporate income tax rate has been cut aggressively. From 21 per cent in 2008, the rate is scheduled to drop yearly until it reaches 15 per cent by January 2012—half its 2000 level. Capital taxes on corporations have been eliminated at the federal level, and the provinces are following suit. Capital cost allowances on capital equipment have been extended to Canadian firms at a deduction level of 50 per cent through to 2011, encouraging businesses to purchase productivity-enhancing equipment at this crucial juncture in the business cycle. The plan calls for the marginal effective tax rate on capital investment to fall to 18.9 per cent by 2013—down dramatically from the nearly 29 per cent rate in 2008!

By the end of the 2007–08 fiscal year, Canadians were happily sitting atop a nearly $10-billion annual surplus—the eleventh federal fiscal surplus in as many years.

Furthermore, tariffs on imported equipment used in production have been eliminated, some personal income tax rates have been reduced, and some sensible new tax credits (such as the working income tax credit) have been introduced. All in all, the federal government has used tax policy effectively.

At the provincial level, Canadians have also seen some well-considered tax reform measures. In response to concerns about deficits and net provincial debt, Quebec has opted to raise its sales tax by 1 percentage point, effective January 1, 2011, while another 1 percentage point increase is in the cards for 2012. Nova Scotia has also acted to lift the provincial portion of its harmonized sales tax by 2 percentage points. Ontario and British Columbia opted to harmonize their provincial sales taxes with the federal GST base under a comparable framework—a move that will generate more revenues as the economic recovery solidifies.

However, tax reform is only one part of the fiscal puzzle. The Canadian fiscal policy landscape has arguably been dominated by overspending in the good times. Politicians have tended to focus on the "here and now" rather than on the country's future economic well-being. Virtually all federal and provincial jurisdictions in Canada offered some form of consumer-based stimulus in the lead-up to the financial crisis, with little thought given to the long-term fiscal sustainability of such measures. This occurred at a time when core public spending was ballooning, while the tax base was remaining fairly flat. One example of the key challenges facing the provinces is health care, which currently absorbs about 41 per cent of total program spending among the provinces collectively. This "core" need is at severe risk of crowding out other program spending as the baby-boom generation ages. These structural problems must be addressed head-on, but have been largely ignored so far.

> **Health care currently absorbs about 41 per cent of total program spending among the provinces collectively.**

As it recovers from the recession, Canada finds itself in relatively good fiscal shape in comparison with many other developed economies. Many nations—developed and developing alike—will be hard-pressed to implement productivity-enhancing tax reform while also returning to fiscal balance in a timely fashion. Canada has responded to the challenge by rebalancing its tax policies in favour of enhanced tax competitiveness going forward; the federal budget for 2010–11 provided a concrete plan for getting back to fiscal balance by 2015–16. However, the "elephant in the room" remains the gap between core program spending and tax revenues.

SHORT-TERM STIMULUS TO BRIDGE THE GAP IN PRIVATE SECTOR DEMAND

Government stimulus through aggressive fiscal and monetary policy intervention is a powerful instrument for restoring economic growth, but it also has its limits. Government stimulus comes in two basic forms: monetary stimulus, through cuts to interest rates and other financial interventions; and fiscal stimulus, through tax cuts and new spending initiatives (which usually result in budgetary deficits that have to be addressed once economic growth returns).

Monetary authorities around the globe intervened aggressively during the winter of 2008–09 to try to stave off a prolonged recession and to address the spectre of generalized deflation (a drop in the overall price index that can create a self-perpetuating downward spiral in consumer spending). Central banks everywhere cut interest rates deeply, with the U.S. Federal Reserve Board and the Bank of Canada reducing short-term rates virtually to zero. The Fed is likely to keep rates at historic lows through to the end of 2010 and into 2011, and the Bank of Canada will proceed carefully in raising Canadian interest rates. The Fed (and many other central banks, but not the Bank of Canada) also resorted to "quantitative easing"—the creation of money, which is then used to buy government bonds—to further fuel the recovery by adding extra monetary stimulus to the U.S. economy.

The Canadian fiscal policy landscape has arguably been dominated by overspending in the good times.

However, the severity of the recession placed limits on monetary stimulus. Commercial banks needed to restore their own financial health before passing the full benefit of lower interest rates on to their customers. Credit markets are healing but are still not back to normal. Because monetary policy works with a long lag, governments could not wait for monetary accommodation to become effective. Fiscal stimulus was therefore required as a complement to monetary action.

In an attempt to turn the tide on what threatened to be a very long and deep recession, governments around the world opened the floodgates of fiscal stimulus. The U.S. came up with a massive fiscal stimulus package and urged fellow governments of the G20 to follow suit. Even the International Monetary Fund (IMF)—traditionally the bastion of fiscal prudence—recommended that countries inject fiscal stimulus worth 2 per cent of GDP. All in all, the G20 countries have gone beyond the call of duty, introducing stimulus packages averaging 2 per cent of GDP in 2009 and 1.5 per cent in 2010. (See Table 2.)

Table 2
Stimulus Plans in the G20
(per cent of GDP)

	2009	2010
Argentina	1.5	0.0
Australia	2.1	1.7
Brazil	0.6	0.8
Canada	1.9	1.7
China	3.1	2.7
France	0.7	0.8
Germany	1.6	2.0
India	0.6	0.6
Indonesia	1.3	0.6
Italy	0.2	0.1
Japan	2.4	1.8
South Korea	3.9	1.2
Mexico	1.5	1.0
Russia	4.1	1.3
Spain	2.3	0.0
Saudi Arabia	3.3	3.5
South Africa	1.8	−0.6
Turkey	0.8	0.3
United Kingdom	1.4	−0.1
United States	2.0	1.8
Weighted average	**2.0**	**1.5**

Source: International Monetary Fund.

Not to be left on the sidelines (or risk being accused of not doing its part), the Canadian government announced a major fiscal stimulus package of its own in January 2009. The plan, designed to kick-start the economy and restore confidence, was billed as providing fiscal stimulus of 1.9 per cent of real GDP in 2009 and 1.7 per cent for 2010, in line with the G20 average.[2]

Attempting to turn the tide on the recession, governments around the world opened the fiscal stimulus floodgates.

FOUR BROAD CATEGORIES OF FISCAL STIMULUS

Fiscal stimulus programs can largely be grouped into four broad categories: temporary tax cuts, permanent tax cuts, tax credits on the purchase of specific items, and spending on infrastructure. Each of these categories uses a wide range of specific measures, and each comes with its own set of benefits and drawbacks. (One of the most effective ways to deliver stimulus in a timely fashion is through the social safety net with its automatic stabilizers, such as Employment Insurance and social assistance. But these programs were already in place and so do not fall into the category of new, active stimulus measures.)

While there was near-universal adoption of stimulus programs around the globe, economists remain divided about the effectiveness of active fiscal measures in reducing the damaging effects of the global recession. A key issue in such circumstances is timing: Will the programs support economic activity while the private sector is still weak? Or will they arrive too late and add to inflationary pressures at a time when the private sector is recovering? Aware of the challenge, governments tried to design their programs to get traction from the new measures as quickly as possible. Programs included such innovations as the "cash for clunkers" program (which encouraged people to replace their older autos with new models), the home renovation tax credit, tax cuts, and spending on small and large infrastructure projects.

---

2   International Monetary Fund, *The State of Public Finances.*

According to the IMF, about one-third of the G20's stimulus efforts are in the form of tax cuts, some of them temporary. In the United States, half of the 2009 stimulus consisted of tax cuts to individuals and corporations; in 2010, this percentage rose to 80 per cent.

Temporary tax cuts can be implemented rapidly, putting cash into the hands of the private sector, be it households or businesses. However, during an economic crisis, the extra funds might be saved rather than spent, especially if the measures are known to be temporary. Recent U.S. evidence suggests that temporary tax cuts had little success in lifting consumer spending. Most of the $100 billion in tax rebates sent to households in early 2008, and credits handed out again in 2009, ended up being added to household savings rather than spending. (See Chart 1.)

Funds flowing to households from permanent tax measures are more likely to be spent. However, permanent tax cuts also result in a permanent loss in government revenues. Inevitably, spending cuts are needed in

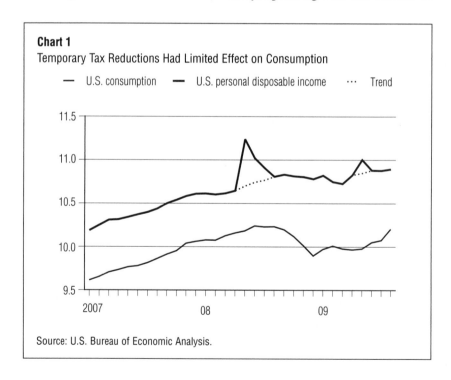

Chart 1
Temporary Tax Reductions Had Limited Effect on Consumption

Source: U.S. Bureau of Economic Analysis.

order to rebalance the budget once the economy recovers. In addition to the uneven impact between permanent and temporary tax cuts, tax measures are also plagued by significant economic leakages. Canada, in particular, is a highly open economy that is deeply integrated into the North American production chain. International trade represents about 40 per cent of Canada's GDP (unlike in the United States, where international trade accounts for just 13 per cent of GDP). As such, about 40 per cent of the impact of every dollar handed back to consumers in Canada via tax cuts will "leak" out of the Canadian economy through increased imports.

Tax credits applied to specific items, such as vehicles or homes, proved effective during the downturn. The U.S. cash-for-clunkers program was surprisingly effective at lifting vehicle sales in July and August 2009. And an $8,000 tax credit for first-time homebuyers in the United States is credited with lifting sales (although many potential buyers appear to have waited until the very last minute to take advantage of the program, which expired at the end of November 2009). Similar, but much less generous, programs were adopted by the Canadian government in its January 2009 budget. Not surprisingly, the impacts of these measures (for example, a $750 tax credit for first-time homebuyers) were much lighter than what we saw in the United States.

> **About 40 per cent of the impact of every dollar handed back to consumers in Canada via tax cuts will "leak" out of the Canadian economy through increased imports.**

Overall, this type of stimulus has proven to be effective and timely, especially if the incentives are large. However, the measures are biased to specific goods or industries, and they can also suffer from significant leakages. A cash-for-clunkers program in Canada, for example, would have bolstered auto imports and produced only a muted impact on the Canadian economy.

The leakages from new infrastructure spending are usually much smaller, depending on the type of project. When completed, infrastructure projects can add to economic output, lower business costs, reduce commute times, and bolster productivity. The problem with infrastructure projects is that they usually take a long time to get started and often require long construction times. Moreover, infrastructure spending will benefit certain sectors, such as construction, more than others. Policy-makers are challenged to balance their choices between quick (yet leaky) tax cuts and slow (but effective) infrastructure spending.

SPECIFIC MEASURES UNDERTAKEN IN CANADA

Like many other governments, the Canadian government has resorted to a wide array of measures in an effort to spread the risks and benefits of stimulus spending. There are often unintended consequences to policy decisions, and it is prudent for governments not to place all of their eggs in one basket. In Canada, the federal stimulus plan came later than did stimulus plans in other G20 nations and was more heavily weighted to infrastructure spending. The federal government promised to increase funding for infrastructure by almost $12 billion, with funds allotted to four key priorities: provincial, territorial, and municipal infrastructure; First Nations infrastructure; knowledge infrastructure (to modernize universities and colleges); and federal infrastructure. The increase in infrastructure spending was expected to be matched by $8.9 billion in provincial contributions, bringing the total stimulus from new infrastructure spending to $20.7 billion over the 2009–10 and 2010–11 fiscal years.

Not surprisingly, the increase in Canadian infrastructure spending has been difficult to coordinate. Spending was not expected to peak until early 2011, long after the economic recovery had begun. Nevertheless, because private investment in structures remained very weak even after the recovery had gotten under way, the federal stimulus program was still timely, helping to bridge the gap until a recovery in private sector investment became more firmly entrenched.

TAX MEASURES

On the tax side, the Canadian government's personal and corporate tax cuts were timely but modest. And due to leakages through savings and imports, they did little to shore up economic growth. Still, overall real government spending in the economy, including infrastructure, is estimated to have increased by 5.1 per cent in 2009. By comparison, in 2008, real government spending grew by 4.1 per cent. Even though infrastructure spending will continue to ramp up, total real government spending was expected to expand by a lesser 4.8 per cent in 2010. And because nearly half of total government spending[3] in the economy accrues to public sector wages, recent clawbacks in wage growth have offset some of the stimulus.

INFRASTRUCTURE MEASURES

Of all the fiscal stimulus measures, infrastructure spending has the largest impact on economic growth. In fact, the Conference Board estimates that in an economy performing below potential, every dollar spent on infrastructure serves to increase Canada's real GDP by as much $1.20.[4] Critics suggest that delays in implementation mean spending usually occurs when the economy starts to recover, and it can crowd out private investment through higher interest rates and higher business construction prices. But in the current business cycle, Canada's stimulus will prove to be timely—even though peak spending on infrastructure occurs in early 2011.

---

3   Excluding transfers to households, businesses, and other levels of government, and debt financing.

4   The economic multiplier is defined as the ratio of the total economic impact from a particular investment or fiscal stimulative measure to the initial value of that investment or measure. In this case, the multiplier is greater than unity, which suggests that the overall impact on GDP will be larger than the value of the spending on infrastructure.

Increases in infrastructure spending began showing up in the second quarter of 2009. Nevertheless, significant slack has built up in the economy, and it will take years to work off. According to Conference Board estimates, the recession created a 5 per cent output gap (the difference between actual and potential output) in 2009. Structural problems, especially those affecting Canada's southern neighbour, will prevent the output gap from closing until late in 2013. Furthermore, real business investment is estimated to have dropped by close to $40 billion in 2009, removing 3.6 per cent from real GDP. With corporations working to improve their balance sheets, no significant recovery in business investment is expected before 2011.

> **Of all the fiscal stimulus measures, infrastructure spending has the largest impact on economic growth.**

Despite its late arrival, government infrastructure spending will have gone a long way toward offsetting the impacts of the recession. In fact, increased infrastructure spending alone is estimated to have contributed about 0.4 per cent to overall economic growth in 2009. And as the spending escalated, it provided another 0.5 per cent boost to real GDP growth in 2010.

ECONOMIC IMPACT ANALYSIS OF TAX MEASURES

Although the income tax measures announced in the federal Economic Action Plan in January 2009 were timelier than the infrastructure spending program, they have a smaller impact on total economic growth. The Conference Board estimates that the economic multiplier on personal income tax cuts is only 0.4 in the first year, while the corporate income tax cut multiplier is even smaller at 0.3. This means that for every dollar spent cutting taxes, real GDP is expected to increase by only 40 cents for personal income tax cuts and 30 cents for corporate income tax cuts. The multiplier on tax cuts is relatively small, as some of the impact is siphoned off through higher imports and savings. This multiplier can be increased somewhat if tax cuts are focused on low-income earners who have a higher propensity to consume.

Altogether, the federal tax package aimed at households and businesses was worth about $5.9 billion in 2009–10 and $3.5 billion in 2010–11 on a net basis, and was scattered across a variety of different measures. On the personal side, the measures included a permanent increase in the basic personal, spousal, and eligible dependant amounts; an increase in the dollar ceiling for the first two personal income tax brackets; a bump to the income levels on which the Canada Child Tax Benefit is based; and an enhancement to the Working Income Tax Benefit. As well, the government increased the Age Credit available to Canadians 65 years of age and older, and it raised the income level at which the Age Credit is fully phased-out. On the corporate side, the government increased the level of small business income eligible for the small business tax rate, and it introduced a temporary 100 per cent capital cost allowance. Although these measures were timely, they are expected to add only marginally to real GDP growth over the near term.

Business investment is estimated to have dropped by close to $40 billion in 2009, removing 3.6 per cent from real GDP.

HOME RENOVATION TAX CREDIT

In an attempt to boost residential investment, the federal government created a temporary Home Renovation Tax Credit (HRTC). The HRTC was a 15 per cent credit that applied to spending on home improvement before February 1, 2010. The credit covered eligible expenditures exceeding $1,000 but up to a maximum of $10,000. Many homeowners took advantage of the offer. While it is difficult to disentangle the effects of the program from other factors affecting home repairs and renovations, data for 2009 suggest that real spending on home repairs and renovations did, in fact, post a quick and significant recovery, especially when compared with the slow recovery in new home construction.

EMPLOYMENT INSURANCE: AUTOMATIC STABILIZER

Additional support for the economy came from the Employment Insurance (EI) program, which is an automatic stabilizer. On top of the basic program, the federal government announced more than $1.7 billion in enhancements to EI. These enhancements included a temporary two-year increase in the regular EI benefit entitlement periods by an additional five weeks. As well, work-sharing agreements that pay partial EI benefits to qualifying workers willing to accept a reduced workweek (and thus avoid layoffs) were extended by 14 weeks. And funding for training delivered through the EI program increased significantly. Payments under the program are estimated to have risen $5.6 billion in 2009. Overall, this is expected to add about 0.2 per cent to real GDP growth in 2009.

The federal and provincial governments had generally benefited from a decade-long boom in revenues.

LESSONS LEARNED

Compared with many other countries, Canada was in a strong position heading into the 2008–09 recession. The country's banks and financial institutions were little exposed to risky subprime mortgages. The federal and provincial governments had generally benefited from a decade-long boom in revenues. Households and businesses were enjoying reduced tax burdens. And the Canadian real estate market was balanced (a situation that would help sustain home prices through the business cycle).

Up until 2008, government spending at both the federal and provincial levels was very strong, as governments seemingly tried to keep up with the strong growth in revenues. Times were good, and finance ministers, it could be argued, tended to neglect the importance of fiscal policy as a stabilizer to the economy.

Provincial governments, for example, passed bills committing themselves to maintaining balanced budgets—legislation that, in many cases, had to be quickly revised once the economic downturn struck. Indeed, such legislation, if enforced, would have only served to worsen the effects of the recession.

The recession underlined the fact that automatic stabilizers—such as EI and other social safety net programs—help weaken the impact of downturns in the business cycle. They enable governments to absorb the direct hit on tax revenues that results from the drop in profits, income, and consumption during times of economic duress.

Another lesson highlighted by government efforts to deal with the economic crisis is that fiscal policy can be difficult to implement in ways that are both timely and effective. Tax cuts, for example, can be given out quickly, but the impact on the economy tends to be muted and short-lived. On the other hand, infrastructure spending provides a lot of "bang for the buck," with the trade-off being that it is often difficult to implement in a timely way.

A highly accommodative monetary policy and fiscal stimulus mitigated the worst of the recession in Canada.

The 2008–09 recession was very deep and worrisome for policymakers around the globe. The call by the IMF for stimulus spending of 2 per cent of GDP was exceptional and did not go unheeded. Canada stepped up to the plate with a stimulus program comparable to that of many other G20 countries. Federal and provincial governments generally opted to devote the bulk of their economic stimulus to infrastructure spending. Even though the impact of infrastructure spending peaks only in early 2011, it is still timely and necessary, given the depressed state of private physical investment.

The stimulus plan helped Canada return to economic growth in the third quarter of 2009, ending a downturn that saw the Canadian economy shrink by a total of 3.2 per cent, peak to trough. As recessions go, this one was less devastating than those in the recent past. The declines in output and employment, for example, were steeper during the 1991 recession, and much steeper still in the 1981–82 recession. Fiscal policy can take at least some of the credit for the turnaround, particularly by helping to close the output gap moving forward as the large fiscal stimulus package ramps up. Along with a highly accommodative monetary policy, fiscal stimulus mitigated the worst of the recession in Canada.

LESSON 2

Recession Only Delayed the Inevitable Workforce Shortages

by *Pedro Antunes* and *Alicia Macdonald*

HIGHLIGHTS

- From peak to trough, the Canadian economy shed approximately 417,000 jobs—a 2.4 per cent drop—during the recession.
- Even though the economy shed many jobs through this cycle, there is no escaping the fundamental force affecting labour markets in Canada—the impending mass exodus of boomers.
- The recession provided only a temporary reprieve from the tight labour market conditions of 2007 and much of 2008. Current and looming skill shortages have implications for labour market and immigration policies and practice.

Employment held up relatively well in Canada, until autumn 2008. That was in marked contrast to the United States, where employment had declined steadily since the beginning of 2008. Once the recession took hold, however, the contraction in real GDP and employment in both countries was fast and furious. From peak to trough, or more specifically, over the nine months from October 2008 to July 2009, the Canadian economy shed about 417,000 jobs—a 2.4 per cent drop.

How was the pain distributed across the economy? The recession did not affect labour markets equally across the country or across different sectors of the economy. The manufacturing, resources, and construction industries saw the largest contractions in production and employment.

And the toll was hardest on young men, especially those working in lower-skilled occupations. In response to slack labour market conditions, many individuals were forced to create their own jobs, resulting in a surge in self-employment. Public sector employment remained stable through the business cycle, and retirement plans for those with defined benefit pensions have not been strongly affected by the general loss in wealth. When it comes to employment, older, experienced workers were largely spared the negative effects of the recession—providing a glimpse of just how tight labour markets for this cohort might get as baby boomers start to retire in earnest. Even though the economy shed many jobs through this cycle, there is no escaping the fundamental force affecting labour markets in Canada—the impending mass exodus of boomers. And there is little evidence that the recession will have a lasting impact on any plans to hold off on retirement.[1]

Yet, when one considers how damaging the recession was on a global basis, the toll on Canadian labour markets was relatively mild. (See Chart 1.) Among the major industrialized economies, job losses in Canada were less painful than in any other country except for Australia and France.

As the economy emerged from the recession, the Canadian labour market stabilized. Job growth resumed in the summer of 2009 and has been especially vigorous since the start of 2010. Although jobs were lost from November 2008 to July 2009, monthly job growth was generally positive after that; and by August 2010, total employment in Canada had returned nearly to its pre-recession peak.[2] Overall, if the recovery continues to progress as expected, the impact of the recession on real GDP and jobs will have been much softer than was the case with the 1981–82 recession, or the 1991–92 recession. (See Chart 2.) Nevertheless, private

---

1   During the recession, we surveyed Canadians about this issue and found that many had decided to delay their retirement because of the effects of the recession on their savings. However, empirical studies suggest that over the longer term, the average age of retirement is not affected by business cycles.

2   It is important to note that labour markets had not returned to normal in August 2010. The economy was still suffering from under-employment, part-time employment remained elevated, and private sector job creation had not yet gained much traction.

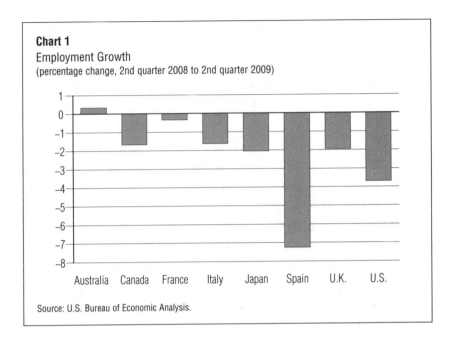

Chart 1

Employment Growth

(percentage change, 2nd quarter 2008 to 2nd quarter 2009)

Source: U.S. Bureau of Economic Analysis.

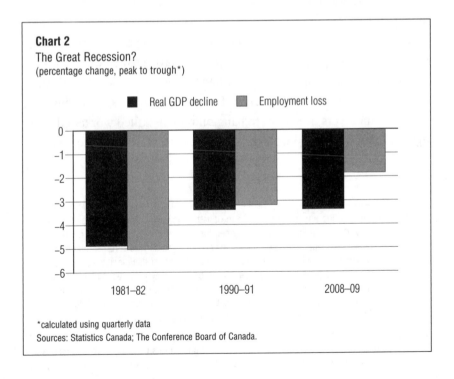

Chart 2

The Great Recession?

(percentage change, peak to trough*)

*calculated using quarterly data

Sources: Statistics Canada; The Conference Board of Canada.

sector firms want to be sure that demand for their goods and services is firmly entrenched before they take on additional payroll commitments. Canada's unemployment rate—a key driver of real wages—will only slowly get back to the "full employment" level of around 6 per cent.

In retrospect, the impact of the 2008–09 recession on employment was much less harsh than past recessions. This is partly due to a fundamental transformation over the past decade that brought Canada's labour market from one in which there was an excess *supply* of labour, to one in which there is excess *demand* for labour—at least among some occupations and in some regions.[3] The unemployment rate reached its recession peak of 8.7 per cent in August 2009. In contrast, the average unemployment rate over the 1980s was 9.4 per cent, and over the 1990s, an abysmal 9.6 per cent! The situation today is far different. The retirement of the baby-boom cohort is just getting under way, and employers are (or should be) well aware of the fundamental forces that are causing a steady erosion in the growth in the labour supply.

No doubt, job losses resulted in temporary slackness in Canada's labour market, and the effect is perhaps compounded by boomers temporarily delaying their retirements due to the plunge in stock markets. But even as the ranks of the unemployed have grown, the supply of workers in some occupations and skilled trades remains slim. According to results from The Conference Board of Canada's compensation survey,[4] employers tried hard to hang onto their skilled workers despite the harsh economic environment—and job losses to date corroborate this finding.

---

3   By our estimates, the unemployment rate in Canada was very close to its absolute minimum in 2006 and 2007. The minimum unemployment rate—or the "natural rate"—is not observable but is estimated, and represents the situation in which the economy is at full employment. Even at full employment, there is a minimum level of unemployment that persists because of structural factors, such as people who are unemployed because they are in transition between jobs, while others may prefer not to work at the current wage. Although the national unemployment rate was close to the natural rate, labour markets were still slack across some occupations and regions, while they were very tight across other occupations and regions.

4   The Conference Board of Canada's 2010 annual compensation survey found that 54 per cent of the 426 organizations that responded had trouble attracting and retaining talent. While this share is down from what was reported in recent years, it remains remarkably high, given the recession.

IMPACTS BY INDUSTRY

Manufacturing was the sector hit hardest by the recession. This industry was already suffering from the competitive pressures brought about by the surging Canadian dollar and had been shedding workers steadily since 2004. By October 2008, manufacturing payrolls were already down 340,000 from their 2004 peak. And then conditions worsened. The bottom fell out of U.S. demand for consumer goods, especially autos—and another 209,000 jobs were lost in just nine months! (See Chart 3.)

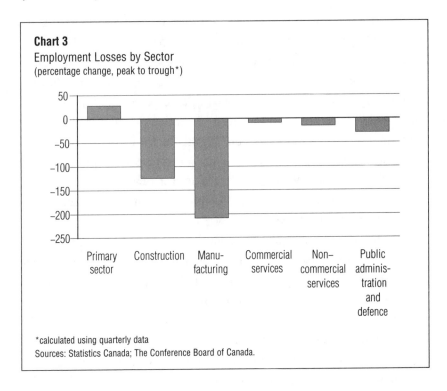

Chart 3
Employment Losses by Sector
(percentage change, peak to trough*)

*calculated using quarterly data
Sources: Statistics Canada; The Conference Board of Canada.

Canada's economy was not only affected by the direct drop in global demand for our goods, but also by the secondary effects of falling commodity prices. While many resource prices have partially recovered, the sharp reduction in commodity prices that began in autumn 2008 saw overall raw material prices drop 22 per cent in 2009. This removed a huge source of cash flow from Canada's capital-intensive energy and resource industries. Coupled with tight credit conditions and falling domestic demand, Canadian businesses held back on capital investment like never before. Total private, real non-residential investment in 2009 posted the sharpest annual decline—down nearly 20 per cent—on record. (Comparable data are available back to 1962.)

> **The toll on employment resulting from the decline in real GDP was much less harsh than in past recessions.**

The impact was felt sharply by Canada's construction workers. Between October 2008 and July 2009, nearly 125,000 jobs were lost in this sector. Job losses hit unskilled workers the hardest; upward wage pressures remained strong for many of the skilled trades in the construction industry.[5]

The primary sector itself also shed a large percentage of its workforce—nearly 4.2 per cent. In terms of numbers, however, the losses are lighter at about 28,000. In general, this sector is highly productive and capital intensive, such that production can be cut significantly with little effects on jobs. With global demand for raw materials recovering, the turnaround in output and employment in the primary sector was already well under way by early 2010.

The booming economy of recent years allowed the creation of a high number of jobs in commercial services. This sector is large and incorporates a wide range of private sector industries—including retail, transportation, utilities, financial, engineering and other professional services, and computer system design (to name just a few). In 2007, commercial services accounted for about 54 per cent of jobs in Canada. Luckily, job losses across commercial services were very light in comparison with previous recessions. From October 2008 to July 2009, the

---

5   Average hourly wages of older workers in the construction sector continued to advance strongly, despite the recession.

commercial services sector shed just 9,000 jobs. That works out to a loss of about 0.1 per cent (although total job losses do partly conceal a shift from full-time to part-time work).

If government policy is meant to be countercyclical, then maintaining public sector jobs during a recession is likely good policy. Interestingly, though, employment in non-commercial services (largely made up of health care and education) declined during the worst of the recession (although only by 15,000), as provincial governments tried to rein in operational spending in response to a drastic decline in revenues. Moreover, employment in public administration and defence also declined, with about 30,000 jobs shed during the nine months to July 2009. While employment in public administration and defence continued to grow in 2009, up 0.1 per cent, this is far shy of the 7 per cent gain registered in 2008.

In 2007, commercial services accounted for about 54 per cent of jobs in Canada. Luckily, job losses across commercial services were very light in comparison with what we've seen in previous recessions.

Over the medium term, governments have already promised to hold back on public sector payrolls (jobs and wages) in an effort to control costs and bring deficits back into balance. Such targets may be difficult to meet. In particular, due to the aging of the baby-boomer cohort, demand for health-care services is rising and attrition resulting from the retirement of health-care workers and public servants is high. As a result, pressure on wages will remain elevated even if job growth is softer going forward.

IMPACTS BY PROVINCE

The sharp declines in manufacturing and natural resource employment during the recession were reflected in the performance of provincial labour markets, with Ontario, British Columbia, Alberta, and Newfoundland and Labrador posting the largest declines in employment. (See Chart 4.) In B.C., the forestry and manufacturing sectors were hit hard by the U.S. housing market crash, causing the province's workforce to shrink by 2.6 per cent in the year leading up to the third quarter of 2009. After reaching historic lows of just over 4 per cent in late 2007 and early 2008, B.C.'s unemployment rate shot up by about 4 percentage points during the recession.

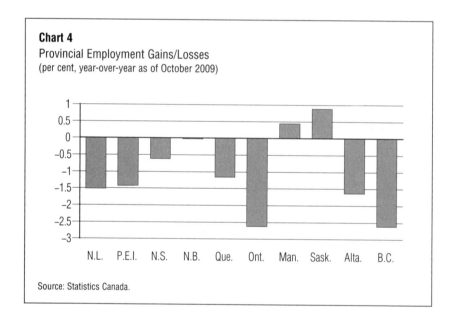

Chart 4
Provincial Employment Gains/Losses
(per cent, year-over-year as of October 2009)

Source: Statistics Canada.

Ontario did not fare much better. Employment fell 2.6 per cent in the year leading up to the third quarter of 2009 as the province's automobile manufacturing industry grappled with a steep drop in U.S. vehicle sales. Ontario's unemployment rate increased by nearly 3 percentage points—from an average of 6.3 per cent over the first half of 2008, to an average of 9.2 per cent over the second half of 2009. At the same time, employment in Quebec fell 1.2 per cent. Quebec's economy did experience a recession, but it was not as deep as in Ontario, thanks to the relatively strong performance of its domestic economy.

Over the same period, Alberta shed about 1.6 per cent of its workforce. But the province's overall loss of about 33,000 jobs understates the effect on labour income; the province actually lost double that number of full-time jobs during the recession. The unemployment rate in Alberta averaged 7 per cent over the second half of 2009—a level that seemed impossible just a few years earlier when labour was such a scarce commodity in the province.

In contrast, labour markets in Manitoba and Saskatchewan came through the recession relatively unscathed, with employment posting modest gains of 0.4 per cent and 0.9 per cent, respectively, from the third quarter of 2008 to the third quarter of 2009. Manitoba suffered a decline in real GDP in 2009 of only 0.2 per cent, which sheltered its labour market. In Saskatchewan, economic growth was hit hard by declines in potash production. However, the potash industry has a very high productivity rate. Consequently, employment losses in the industry were mild compared with the decline in output.

Labour markets in Nova Scotia and New Brunswick also held up relatively well through the recession. Output growth fell in both provinces in 2009, but the recessions were mild. From the third quarter of 2008 to the third quarter of 2009, employment in Nova Scotia fell by 0.6 per cent, in line with the decline in GDP. In New Brunswick, government investment and tax cuts helped mitigate the impact on the labour market, with total employment remaining flat through the recession. Government stimulus helped Prince Edward Island avoid a recession. Even so, employment in the province declined by 1.4 per cent between the third quarter of 2008 and the third quarter of 2009.

Newfoundland and Labrador's economy was battered by declining oil and gas extraction, a strike at the Voisey's Bay nickel mine, and shrinking demand for newsprint. As a result, the provincial economy contracted by 10.2 per cent in 2009. Despite the significant loss in output, the impact on the labour market was muted by a still-strong domestic economy. Between the third quarter of 2008 and the third quarter of 2009, employment fell by only 1.5 per cent in the province.

IMPACTS BY AGE AND GENDER

Comparatively speaking, women suffered less than men from the effects of the recession. In the nine months up to July 2009, some 312,000 men became unemployed, while only 106,000 women lost their jobs—a three-to-one ratio. This is partly because women over 55 saw their employment levels rise over this period, with gains in commercial services and public sector employment. Older men also saw their employment levels rise—but not to the same extent. The largest cohort in the labour market, accounting for nearly 70 per cent of employment, is made up of men and women aged 25 to 54. This cohort was the most affected by job losses in manufacturing, with male employment once again suffering the biggest drop.

By far, young people were the hardest hit by the recession. Job losses for those aged 15 to 24 totalled 209,000 over the nine months to July 2009. That means 50 per cent of all job losses were borne by a cohort that accounts for only 15 per cent of the workforce. Once again, men (many of them construction workers) were hardest hit, with employment in this group declining by 138,000 and their unemployment rate skyrocketing over 5 percentage points to reach 18.5 per cent at its peak.

RECESSION AND THE RETIREMENT DECISION

Going forward, the single most important factor shaping the labour market over the next two decades will be the retirement of the baby-boom cohort. The first members of this cohort were reaching retirement age just as equity markets around the world tumbled. As a result, many boomers were forced to examine whether to go ahead with their retirement plans or to hold off on retirement until their stock market losses were at least partially recouped.[6]

If boomers were to delay their retirement, it would provide some short-term reprieve to the projected slowdown in labour supply growth.

While the Toronto Stock Exchange composite index has rebounded strongly from its March 2009 low, it remains well below the peak reached in May 2008, and equity market performance in 2010 has been bumpy. The Conference Board had previously conducted an econometric analysis of the key factors that determine retirement age and found that expected retirement income (approximated using net financial assets per employee) had a significant impact on the retirement decision.[7] From the first quarter of 2008 to the first quarter of 2009, net financial assets per employee fell by 15 per cent. While net financial assets per employee have shown some recent strength, it will likely be a while before losses are fully recouped.

Many boomers may have decided to postpone retirement until their stock market losses are at least partially recouped.

Two studies on the impact of the 2008–09 recession on retirement decisions in the U.S. (where the recession was longer and much deeper) suggest that the recession will have neither a significant nor lasting impact on retirement decisions. One study found that if the decline in the stock market resulted in people delaying retirement, the likely duration would be only a few months—not a few years.[8] And using U.S. data, the second study found that long-run stock market fluctuations do affect retirement decisions—but only for the highly educated group in the 62- to 69-age group. The authors conclude that when looking at all potential retirees, retirement rates would actually rise. That's because the increase

6   In a January 2010 survey, the Conference Board found that about one-third of households headed by someone aged 45 to 64 planned to delay their retirement by at least a year.

7   The Conference Board of Canada, "The Determinants of the Retirement Decision."

8   Gustman, Steinmeier, and Tabatabai, "How Do Pension Changes Affect Retirement Preparedness?"

in the number of involuntary retirements due to sluggish labour market conditions would exceed the number of postponed retirements.[9] For example, among older workers, an extended layoff could easily turn into an unwanted early retirement.

In the Canadian context, we expect the impact of delayed retirement on the labour market will be even lighter. Losses in the stock market have generally been more moderate than in the U.S., while home prices—an important non-financial asset for many households—held up well through the recession. Even if some boomers decide to delay retirement, it will likely be for only a short period of time. As such, the recession will not generate a significant boost to labour supply. Furthermore, an increase in retirement due to job losses and the encouragement of early retirement may have an offsetting effect—decreasing labour supply relative to what was forecast prior to the downturn.

POCKETS OF LABOUR MARKET TIGHTNESS PERSIST

A considerable amount of slack has appeared in Canadian labour markets since the recession first struck. Data from the Conference Board's *Compensation Outlook 2010* showed that the percentage of employers who were experiencing difficulty attracting and retaining talent had fallen significantly. (See Chart 5.) In 2008, 74 per cent of respondents nationally said they were having difficulty finding and retaining talent. In 2009, the proportion had declined 20 percentage points to 54 per cent.

Over the two previous years, 100 per cent of compensation outlook survey respondents in the resource sector reported challenges attracting and retaining staff; but in 2009, that number dropped to 57 per cent. Additionally, only 50 per cent of private sector employers reported challenges in 2009, down from 73 per cent the previous year. Regionally, labour markets remain tightest in the Prairies where 85 per cent of Saskatchewan employers and 77 per cent of Manitoban employers

---

9   Colie and Levine, *Will the Current Economic Crisis Lead to More Retirements?*

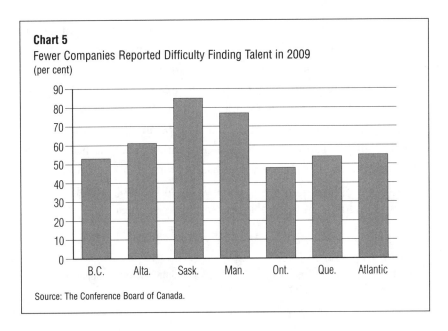

Chart 5
Fewer Companies Reported Difficulty Finding Talent in 2009
(per cent)

Source: The Conference Board of Canada.

reported difficulties retaining and attracting staff. (See Chart 6.) With labour relatively abundant, survey respondents have held back on wage growth, reporting an average non-union pay increase of 2.4 per cent in 2009. Planned increases in 2010 for non-union employees are expected to come in slightly higher at 2.7 per cent.

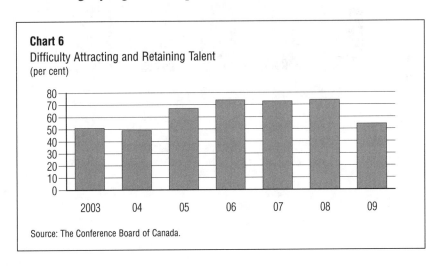

Chart 6
Difficulty Attracting and Retaining Talent
(per cent)

Source: The Conference Board of Canada.

For some occupations, there has been no reprieve from tight labour market conditions—strong wage growth and difficulties in finding qualified personnel remain the norm. Chart 7 illustrates a sample of scarce-skill professions that continued to experience low unemployment rates throughout the economic downturn. In addition to these low unemployment rates, there is the challenge of an aging workforce—a challenge that is especially acute in occupations such as health care, management, and the skilled trades. Such professions will continue to suffer labour supply shortages, and will be particularly affected by the pending retirement of baby boomers in the years ahead.

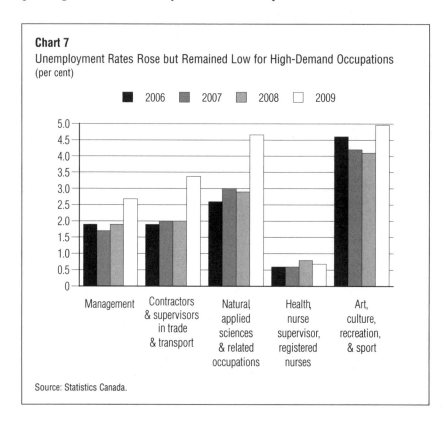

Chart 7
Unemployment Rates Rose but Remained Low for High-Demand Occupations
(per cent)

Source: Statistics Canada.

LESSONS LEARNED

Unskilled Youths Have the Most to Lose

Because the recession did not hit all industries equally, the impacts on different age and gender cohorts were also mixed. Moreover, the fundamental causes of the decline in labour force growth are the aging of the population and the resulting increase in retirements, which reduces the supply of workers who are generally higher up the skills and pay scales. The combination of these factors had the greatest impact on younger and less-skilled workers—and, in particular, on men.

> **Cohorts with higher education had lower unemployment rates, higher labour force participation rates, and better wages.**

The pre-recession boom in resource sector investment and construction provided many opportunities for youths to enter the workforce— in many cases prematurely. But the opportunities abruptly came to an end, and many young people have chosen to upgrade their skills in order to re-enter the labour market. Moreover, men are under-represented in colleges and universities in Canada, leaving them more vulnerable to an economy that continues to transition from a low- to a high-skilled workforce. Skills development and financial support for the retraining of younger unskilled workers should remain a key priority for business leaders and policy-makers as we recover from the recession. High school dropouts will need to consider a return to school, while college and university programs can expect to see stronger near-term enrolment growth. Getting young people back into the labour force will be a positive development over the long run, especially as these youths upgrade their education and skills. The fundamental story from the data is that cohorts with higher educational attainment had lower unemployment rates, higher labour force participation rates, and better wages.

The Return of Labour Market Tightness

Heading into the recession of 2008–09, Canadian labour markets were incredibly tight. The national unemployment rate had fallen steadily and stood at the Conference Board's estimate of the natural rate.[10] Indeed, across many regions and occupations, there were severe labour shortages, thus creating significant upward pressure on wages. The recession resulted in a significant slackening of the labour market, and it will take a few years before the damage to employment is undone. But even though labour markets slackened overall, many pockets continued to feel the pressure. Highly skilled workers, especially those in public sector occupations, remained in short supply. Over the next few years, as the economy gains strength and the unemployment rate drops back down to its structural low, finding workers while also containing wage pressures will resurface as a key challenge for Canadian employers.

> **Skill shortages have implications for immigration policy and practice, and for temporary and contract workers.**

Over the longer term, labour will become an increasingly scarce commodity as the baby-boom cohort begins to retire in earnest. Despite high immigration rates, source population growth (roughly equal to those aged 15 and over) will remain soft due to low fertility rates and a smaller cohort in the child-bearing years. Slower growth in the source population and declining rates of labour market participation will continue to erode growth in labour supply in the foreseeable future.

---

10   The natural rate of unemployment is the rate that prevails when labour markets are in equilibrium.

CONCLUSION

While labour supply is now plentiful in many industries, the recession provided only a temporary reprieve from the tight labour market conditions of 2007 and much of 2008. Current and looming skill shortages have implications for immigration policy and practice, as well as for the use of temporary and contract workers. In the face of such widespread shortages, succession planning throughout organizations is of paramount importance. Failure to adequately plan for the forthcoming deceleration in labour supply growth will leave organizations facing shortages of the skilled employees they need—a situation that threatens future growth.

LESSON 3
The Financial Sector Is Unique and Needs New Standards

by *Louis Thériault* and *Michael Burt*

HIGHLIGHTS

- The financial sector plays a special role in the economy; it is the only intermediary sector that interacts with every other sector in a market-based economy.
- The extraordinary loss of confidence in the global financial system in the fall of 2008 led to massive interventions by central banks and governments.
- To avoid a repeat event, broad principles for minimum standards and best practices in the financial sector need to be established internationally and put into force locally.

In the fall of 2008, the world economy was on the verge of falling into the worst economic downturn since the 1930s. The world's largest financial institutions found themselves awash in toxic financial assets, and the impact spread like a virus, infecting the international financial system with fear. Thanks to extraordinary efforts by policy-makers, we managed to avoid the worst-case scenario—a financial collapse. But the depth and duration of the recession dictates that a careful assessment of what occurred must take place if we are to prevent it from happening again.

In the case of the financial sector, two specific lessons can be drawn. First, the rapidly cascading sequence of events that followed the bankruptcy of Lehman Brothers in September 2008 reinforced the fact that the financial sector is a cornerstone for every other part of the economy, but also that business and consumer confidence are the cornerstones of the financial system. Second, the regulatory frameworks for the global and national financial systems need a careful and in-depth review and adjustment.

CONFIDENCE IS THE CORNERSTONE

The financial sector plays a special role in the economy. It is the only intermediary sector that interacts with every other sector in a market-based economy. It concentrates financial resources and re-allocates them in a way that enables individuals and businesses to create ongoing wealth and to fuel the economy. No other sector is so fundamental to economic activities; without it, capitalism could not exist.

Paradoxically, the functioning of the financial system is critically dependent on confidence—confidence that savings and investments are secure, confidence that liquidity is available, and confidence that regulation is adequate and respected. A break in confidence can lead to a break in the operation of the financial system. Conversely, a restoration in confidence is critical to restoring the health of the financial system.

The origins of the financial crisis were percolating long before the September 2008 bankruptcy of financial services giant Lehman Brothers. Clear signs appeared as early as 2006, when delinquencies from subprime borrowers began to rise sharply—and then kept rising. The first visible impact from the securitization of these bad mortgages appeared in June 2007 when two hedge funds managed by Bear Stearns reported catastrophic losses. The following month, the funds collapsed completely. Shortly after, the German government bailed out German savings bank Commerzbank, and the U.K. government provided liquidity to keep a British bank, Northern Rock, afloat. Ultimately, the U.K. government had to nationalize Northern Rock. Meanwhile, major international banks started to publicly announce heavy writedowns related to mortgage-backed securities.

The mounting pressure on the financial system had major central banks reacting as early as January 2008,[1] when the U.S. Federal Reserve, the European Central Bank, the Bank of England, the Swiss National Bank, and the Bank of Canada injected liquidity in a concerted effort to facilitate credit. Evidently, the message of rising financial risk had not yet been heard by everyone—stock markets managed to remain fairly optimistic until July 2008. That month, the failure of U.S. mortgage lender IndyMac and the emergency rescue plan for Fannie Mae and Freddie Mac sent a clear signal about the seriousness of the structural damage that had been done.

And then the expected bailout of Lehman Brothers in September 2008—one of the most venerable U.S. financial institutions—never materialized. Lehman went under. Word that the erupting financial crisis had claimed such a high-profile casualty sent a shock wave through the world financial system. Stock markets nosedived, erasing almost 25 per cent of their value in the first week of October alone, as fear ran wild through global financial markets.

Perhaps the most visible signal of the collapse in confidence in the financial system—after the bankruptcy of Lehman Brothers and the effective nationalization of AIG the following day—was the rise in the risk premium that banks charge each other. This can be measured by the spread between the three-month LIBOR (London Interbank Offered Rate) rate and the three-month U.S. T-bill rate, which is often referred to as the TED spread. The TED spread more than doubled in the days immediately following the Lehman bankruptcy and peaked at more than 4 percentage points in mid-October—or more than five times the usual spread. The interbank market was effectively frozen.

This extraordinary loss of confidence resulted in a seizing up of the markets for a variety of financial products and led to massive interventions by central banks. For example, the U.S. Federal Reserve effec-

---

1   In a statement following the meeting of G7 Finance Ministers and Central Bank Governors in Tokyo on February 9, 2008, the participants declared: "Each of us has taken actions, appropriate to our domestic circumstances, in the areas of liquidity provision, monetary policy, and fiscal policy." This shows that some actions had taken place as early as autumn 2007.

tively became the buyer of last resort for commercial paper in order to support this important source of short-term financing. With financial institutions all but unwilling to lend to one another, policy-makers also stepped in to help recapitalize banks and to restore some order to financial markets. Measures included the U.S. Troubled Asset Relief Program (TARP), which provided equity injections from the U.S. government into key money centre banks.

> **Along with the knowledge that the financial system is vital to a market-based economy—and is different from other sectors—comes the need to ensure the system is operated in a responsible way, serving a wider interest.**

The $700-billion TARP was immediately controversial and remains so to this day. Some regarded it as the wrong policy tool to stabilize financial institutions and other companies. Why, some argued, should the government intervene to help private companies that had only themselves to blame for their problems? To some extent, we agree with that sentiment. A purge of the system was indeed needed. These companies had to be held accountable and pay the price for their mismanagement—but not at any cost. The desire to make those responsible pay could not outweigh the need to maintain the stability of the global financial system, and there is little question that the system's stability was threatened at that time. The panic triggered by Lehman Brothers' bankruptcy indicates that confidence had been lost. The global financial system was on the verge of a crisis— perhaps as serious as the one that led to the Great Depression of the 1930s.

A strong message from governments was essential, and TARP and similar programs in other countries were part of the solution. Subsequent concerted efforts by G20 governments and central banks— to re-stabilize specific segments of financial markets and to provide the system with liquidity—sent another clear signal that help was on the way in the form of massive liquidity, record-low interest rates, and stimulus money. Thanks to this massive intervention, banks slowly began once again to lend to each other. Credit conditions relaxed and confidence was on the rebound. The worst-case scenario had been avoided.

This crisis reaffirmed that without confidence, the financial system can crumble—and without the financial system, the economy cannot function. The problems of Wall Street can quickly become those of Main Street if banks are unwilling or unable to lend to businesses and consumers. That is the situation we faced in the autumn of 2008, and public authorities needed to use the nation's balance sheet to intervene in the financial system in a time of crisis in order to restore confidence.

"SMART REGULATION" NEEDED

As the global economy recovers, will obscure financial instruments and high financial leverage once more become the norm and make investors lose sight of the real risk associated with securities? Even without new regulations, it is safe to say that this will probably not occur in the short or medium term. The global economy is recovering, and the current generation of leaders of large financial institutions has learned a painful lesson. However, memories tend to be short, and fundamental rules governing the financial system will have to change to prevent this situation from happening again in the future. Along with the knowledge that the financial system is vital to a market-based economy—and is therefore different than other sectors—comes the need to ensure the system is operated in a responsible way that serves a wider interest. What we need are mechanisms to reduce what is called "systemic risk"—the risk that the whole financial system or an entire market might collapse, as opposed to the risk of failure by any single institution or component of the system.

Changes in key aspects of financial sector regulation are required. Broad principles regarding minimum standards and best practices for capital requirements, transparency, and accounting rules—as well as incentives to implement and follow such rules—must be established internationally and put into force locally.[2]

CAPITAL REQUIREMENTS

Securitization of various debt instruments lay at the core of the financial crisis, and regulators would probably have strong popular support if they were to try to constrain the use of this type of structured financial instrument. But historically, securitization has served consumers and financial institutions well by reducing the cost of loans for consumers and by freeing up capital for institutions, thereby increasing credit availability. The problem was that the associated capital required to support these financial instruments was inadequate. Thus, capital requirements should be increased to better represent the "real" risk underlying various securities. This should be accompanied by more stringent due diligence so as to better understand the risks. As well, issuers of structured products should maintain a larger ongoing exposure to their own products, thereby reducing the incentive for issuers to obfuscate on the contents or understate the risks.

TRANSPARENCY AND ACCOUNTING RULES

Since the securitization of risk remains, in principle, a desirable method of creating financial vehicles, efforts to redesign regulation should focus on rules that enhance the transparency of the risks being securitized. Transparency rules should apply as well to firms' exposure to potential

---

2   Leaders of the G20 are already moving forward on some of these actions, which were identified by the Financial Stability Forum back in autumn 2007. Progress to date on key aspects of the global financial reform is available from the Basel-based Financial Stability Board.

default in these assets. Also, new accounting rules should require hedge funds to report risk positions on their balance sheets on a timely basis. These new rules should help credit rating agencies better assess these new and complex structured products and how they compare with more traditional investments. (The difficulty in rating the risk of these products was a major flaw that contributed to the recent financial crisis.)

INCENTIVE SCHEMES

Compensation incentives for officers in financial institutions are largely driven by short-term returns that often are associated with larger risk taking. This focus on the short term can increase market volatility, inflate trading volumes, and amplify economic cycles. Therefore, financial incentives should be changed so that they reward fund managers based more on their long-term performance and less on short-term results.

These are examples of important ways in which strengthened regulations could make the financial sector more effective. Other critical parts of the regulatory framework that also deserve attention include proper supervision and clearing mechanisms for the huge over-the-counter derivatives market, adequate liquidity requirements, more stringent transparency and accountability rules for credit rating agencies, and better protection for consumers and investors.

Proposed changes by the European Commission, as well as the new U.S. financial regulation reform statute known as the Dodd-Frank Act, largely reflect these ideas. Key elements of the Dodd-Frank Act include:

- increased regulatory oversight of non-bank financial firms (such as hedge funds, private equity funds, and insurance companies), as well as limitations on the ability of banks to invest in these organizations;
- the delineation of clear lines of responsibility among regulators so as to eliminate loopholes and gaps in the system;
- the imposition of a new regulatory regime on trading over-the-counter derivatives, with the goal of increasing transparency and liquidity while reducing systemic risk;

- the creation of a new Office of Credit Ratings at the Securities and Exchange Commission. The office will define new rules for independence and transparency at credit rating agencies; and
- the creation of a Financial Stability Oversight Council, which will have considerable powers to assess and mitigate systemic risks. These powers include the ability to impose capital, leverage, and liquidity requirements that increase as a firm increases in size and, potentially, the power to order the breakup of firms.

NEXT STEPS

The rationale for these proposed and enacted changes to the financial sector regulatory framework is simple: Stricter and clearer rules are required to avoid the ripple effect from the failure of large financial institutions. The overarching lesson provided by the financial crisis is that the world economy faces systemic risk. This term reflects the reality that financial institutions are intertwined in such a way that "[e]ven healthy banks that transact with others may become vulnerable. Failure by a large financial institution can thus cause systemic failure domestically and in other countries."[3] In other words, the failure of banks can create more serious damage to the economy than can failures among most other institutions—and the regulatory framework must reflect this fact.

However, it is not enough to simply add rules and boost spending on bureaucracies. As an illustration, the average real growth in spending on the U.S. federal finance and banking regulatory agencies between 1980 and 2008 was 4 per cent annually,[4] outpacing spending growth at other U.S. federal economic regulatory agencies and real growth in the economy as a whole. But because there were fundamental problems with the financial sector's regulatory framework, increased spending

---

3   Masson and Pattison, *The Financial Crisis, Regulatory Reform, and International Coordination*, 7.

4   de Rugy and Warren, *Regulatory Agency Spending Reaches New Height.*

on regulation alone was not able to prevent the financial crisis. As well, regulators had difficulty keeping up with the pace of innovation in financial products in recent years.

The new U.S. legislation acknowledges this problem, and the extensive streamlining of existing regulations and the better defining of responsibilities among regulatory agencies is welcome. But this reform does not guarantee success—that will ultimately depend on the supervisory and enforcement mechanisms that are put in place alongside the new rules. Without proper supervisory and enforcement capacity, the legislation will not be effective. The new powers given to the U.S. Federal Reserve and the Bank of England[5] are a step in the right direction—but a true assessment of their worth will come only when objective measures of compliance with the new rules are instituted.

A 2009 Conference Board report[6] argued that any changes in financial regulation need to follow the core principle that, rather than try to implement a global or transnational approach, financial reform must leave national regulators in charge of modifying their regulatory framework.

One reason for this approach is that financial crises generally have local origins. The most recent crisis was largely the result of home-grown problems with mortgage lending in the United States. The crisis spread around the globe due to linkages between the U.S. and the rest of the world, such as the heavy involvement of U.S. financial institutions in foreign markets and foreign institutions in the U.S. market. Problems in Europe's housing sector were also a factor. The bursting of the housing bubble—in the U.K. and Spain in particular—acted as an accelerant on a fire that originated in the United States. Thus, early intervention in the U.S. could have significantly reduced the crisis that later occurred.

---

5   The Dodd-Frank Act establishes clear lines of responsibilities among bank regulators and makes the Federal Reserve a "consolidated supervisor" with the mandate of assessing risk throughout the financial system. In England, the proposed new legislation recommends the elimination of the tripartite financial sector supervisory model and a significantly enhanced supervisory role for the Bank of England.

6   Masson and Pattison, *International Financial Policy Reform and Options for Canada.*

Although increased international cooperation is required (given that capital flows criss-cross borders), the creation of a global regulatory body is not a practical solution. In fact, a binding treaty on international finance would be a major break from the long-established practice of cooperation on national guidelines and peer pressure. Reaching a consensus among even the major players in international finance could be near impossible. Instead, broad principles regarding minimum standards and best practices need to be adopted, with the specifics left to individual countries. Among these broad principles:

- Correcting market failures should be done with minimum intervention.
- A list of priorities for action must be drawn up (since not all market failures are equally important).
- The long-term implications of any changes must be fully understood.

CANADA'S ROLE

The impact of the financial crisis in Canada was not as dramatic as it was in other countries. The often-criticized restrictions on the degree of leverage against capital and on foreign investment in the Canadian banking sector have helped maintain a more conservative approach to lending in this country. Also, the proportion of mortgage-backed securities in the portfolios of most large Canadian fund managers was relatively low. With the exception of the Caisse de dépôt et placement du Québec (which suffered serious losses), most institutions escaped relatively unscathed from the brunt of the implosion in value of these toxic financial assets. (The fact that there was no real estate bubble in Canada was also a big help.)

Canada added to its credibility in international financial circles by rapidly demonstrating progress on the suggested reforms (such as on incentive schemes) and by proposing the idea of "embedded contingent capital" to increase capital for banks in financial trouble.[7] This credibility helped Canada convince its G20 partners to drop the idea of introducing a generic bank tax to finance any future bailouts of failing banks.

These actions also helped to make the financial sector stronger and more transparent. More fundamentally, Canada's leadership and credibility strengthen consumer and business confidence in the financial system.

CONCLUSION

The financial sector is different—it is linked to every other segment of the economy and is pivotal to the functioning of a modern market economy. Therefore, it must be treated differently from all other sectors. The shattering of business and consumer confidence at the height of the global financial crisis exemplifies how problems in the financial sector can ripple through many other parts of the global economy. Significant policy intervention by central banks and governments was needed to restore confidence and build a floor under the financial system.

Having taken the necessary steps to restore confidence and stabilize the financial system, policy-makers now need to ensure that a crisis of this magnitude does not happen again. This does not mean that we should create a system in which banks are never allowed to fail. But the massive costs associated with this crisis—in terms of destroyed wealth, higher unemployment, and lost income—create an obligation to act. Broad principles regarding minimum standards and best practices for capital requirements, transparency, and accounting rules—as well as incentives to implement and follow such rules—need to be established internationally and put into force locally.

---

7   For more information on the idea of embedded contingent capital, see remarks by the Superinten-dent of Financial Institutions, Julie Dickson, to the Financial Services Invitational Forum on May 6, 2010. In her remarks, Dickson defines embedded contingent capital as ". . . a security that converts to common equity when a bank is in serious trouble, thereby replenishing the core capital of the bank without the use of taxpayer dollars." See Dickson, "Too Big to Fail and Embedded Contingent Capital."

Leaders of the G20 have agreed on core principles for the international financial reform. New U.S. legislation and proposed changes in Europe are clearly demonstrating that these principles are going beyond rhetoric. However, significant work remains to be done before changes to the regulatory framework are fully deployed. Achieving success hinges on the participation of financial institutions and cooperation among supervisory bodies in the application of new standards among countries. Canada was fortunate to avoid the worst of the financial crisis, and it has taken advantage of its credibility in international financial circles by demonstrating leadership in adopting change. The best way for Canada to ensure that it remains a leader is by continuing to work with other major countries and international bodies, such as the IMF, to improve policy coordination, refine early warning systems, and address policy weaknesses.

LESSON 4
Public Sector Financial Institutions Prove Their Worth

by *Glen Hodgson*

HIGHLIGHTS

- Public sector financial institutions play a critical role as a backstop for the global financial system.

- A key lesson is that once a financial crisis hits, it is too late for governments to create institutional capacity at the global, regional, or national level to provide fall-back credit support—the institutions must already exist.

- These institutions—internationally and in Canada—have proven their collective value as policy tools for shoring up a severely weakened global financial system.

Public sector financial institutions play a critical role as a backstop for the global financial system and for specific countries. Failings in the private financial system were at the root of the crisis and recession. The problem was centred in (but not restricted to) the U.S. and was spread by global distribution channels.

The financial crisis was driven by the lethal combination of over-leveraging of capital, over-extension of credit (especially for subprime mortgages in the U.S.), and the securitization of these unsound credits around the globe. On September 15, 2008, global financial giant Lehman Brothers went under. A number of other key private sector banks and insurers were in deep trouble. The system was at risk.

The Federal Reserve and the U.S. Treasury acted swiftly. They nationalized the country's two largest mortgage entities, Fannie Mae and Freddie Mac, and essentially took over the world's largest insurance company, AIG. They provided share capital to shore up key banks, such as Citigroup and Bank of America. The dramatic moves by the U.S. government and the Fed were desperately needed. The bankruptcy of Lehman led to a panic in the commercial paper, credit-derivative, and bank-funding markets that significantly worsened many banks' balance sheets almost overnight. More generally, the global banking system was pulling back sharply on credit extension to keep banks' balance sheets intact.

Fortunately, the system also contained some well-structured, professionally managed lenders and insurers in the public sector with the capacity to step up and fill gaps in the financial marketplace. In addition to the remarkable intervention by governments to shore up private financial markets, these public sector organizations became part of the policy solution to the systemic risk.

GLOBAL PUBLIC SECTOR FINANCIAL INSTITUTIONS

Some context is required. Just a few years ago—before the financial crisis hit—it was fashionable in some financial and economic circles to ask why many of these public sector financial institutions should continue to exist. At the global level, the International Monetary Fund and the World Bank had seen their roles shrink dramatically through the boom times earlier in the decade. Private capital markets had expanded significantly, and countries were able to access new sources of private capital without turning to the Fund or the Bank.

New annual lending by the IMF to assist countries in distress had fallen sharply. In 2007, only 1.2 billion special drawing rights, or SDRs (about US$1.6 billion), were disbursed to members, and the IMF was cutting staff and expenses. The World Bank continued to provide development finance to poorer developing countries—about $17 billion in 2007—but it was becoming marginalized by private capital flows to the developing world, which had grown significantly over time to surpass $500 billion a year.

What a difference a crisis makes. Since 2008, long-standing public sector financial institutions have added tremendous value by helping to build a floor under a collapsing global credit system.

Neither organization had adapted its governance structure to changes in global economic power fast enough. They needed to find a way to include countries such as China, India, and Brazil in decision making more fully. Otherwise, they risked a further decline in their status, given the dramatic shift in economic growth toward emerging markets over the past two decades. This was particularly true for the IMF.

What a difference a crisis makes. Since 2008, long-standing public sector financial institutions have added tremendous value by helping to build a floor under a collapsing global credit system. On the global stage, the IMF and World Bank—which have had a mandate since 1944 to provide funding for country stabilization and development—were challenged by the financial crisis to step forward as lenders and as policy advisors, just as they had done many times previously. Both met the challenge by committing huge sums to countries hard hit by the crisis. The IMF committed SDR 65.8 billion (about US$100 billion) to 15 countries in crisis in its fiscal year ending April 2009, along with providing policy advice to the G20 and across the global economy. It disbursed significant financial assistance to its members as part of the strategy to restore financial stability—SDR 14 billion in 2008, a further SDR 22 billion in 2009, and SDR 10.7 billion to June 2010. And as the financial crisis has evolved, so too has the IMF's role. In response to the financial crisis in Greece, the IMF played an exceptional role in 2010 by helping the larger eurozone members create a credit backstop of an estimated $1 trillion for eurozone countries in financial difficulty.

The World Bank committed nearly $60 billion in its fiscal year 2009, a 54 per cent increase from the previous year. Commitments have been made, through the G20 process, to give emerging markets a larger ownership share and more influence in decision making in the IMF and World Bank. These institutions are at the centre of the global strategy to restore confidence to markets and rekindle economic growth.

> **A key lesson is that once a financial crisis hits, it is too late for governments to create institutional capacity at the global, regional, or national level to provide fall-back credit support.**

At the national level, governments around the world were compelled to use their national balance sheets directly—via treasuries and central banks—to prop up key private financial institutions and address immediate gaps in their financial systems. Some analysts estimate that the U.S. government alone provided total support to the U.S. financial sector of US$10 trillion at its peak, through a combination of nationalization in whole or in part (e.g., AIG, Fannie Mae, Freddie Mac), equity injections to multiple banks, various guarantees, asset purchases, and bridge financing.

But in many cases, it was neither desirable nor practical for governments to use the blunt instruments of nationalization, equity injections, or direct government guarantees. Expert institutions—where they existed—were often much better placed to help diagnose the problem, provide advice on solutions, and extend credit.

A key lesson is that once a financial crisis hits, it is too late for governments to create institutional capacity at the global, regional, or national level to provide fall-back credit support. The institutions must already exist, with a clear operating mandate, experienced and professional staff, and the financial capacity to respond to the financial needs. Some have called this—having organizations already in operation that can ramp up their operations when the private market fails—the "Sleeping Beauty"[1] or "state of readiness" strategy of global finance.

CANADIAN PUBLIC SECTOR FINANCIAL INSTITUTIONS

A comprehensive assessment of how other global, regional, and national public sector financial institutions responded to the crisis is beyond the scope of this chapter. For Canada, however, we can say that the federal government's financial institutions—specifically the Business Development Bank of Canada (BDC) and Export Development Canada (EDC)—did step up to the plate and provide exceptional credit support in a time of crisis. A third federal financial institution—Farm Credit Canada (FCC)—continues to implement its mandate to provide credit to farms and agri-business, and has seen strong demand for its services. Collectively, these organizations have helped to speed the healing of the Canadian financial system.

There has been recurring debate in Canada about the positioning of the BDC, EDC, and FCC within the Canadian financial marketplace. One approach would see these organizations operate as lenders or insurers of last resort, taking only risks the private sector will not take. This approach would have little or no overlap with the private sector, but it could also be very expensive for the federal government in terms of credit losses.

The federal government considered this approach over the past fifteen years, but essentially rejected it for two reasons. First, a lender or insurer of last resort takes only the worst credit risks, which creates significant financial risk for the national treasury. In earlier decades, the federal government had some unpleasant episodes with the financial Crown corporations, experiences it does not want to repeat. It therefore has chosen to move away from the high-risk model of lender of last resort. Second, there

---

1   A term used by Malcolm Stephens, former head of the British export credit agency, Export Credit Guarantee Department (ECGD).

was a realization over time within the federal government that its three financial institutions could play a larger and more sophisticated role as a complement to private sources of capital. These institutions could share in risk taking with the private market while being present in the marketplace through the entire business cycle. The federal financial institutions could be guided by the concept of "filling gaps." On occasion, they would take on riskier transactions—but selectively, according to clear risk assessment criteria. On other occasions, they could work as a partner or share the risk with private sector institutions to allow a given transaction to be completed. Since governments and their institutions are able to take a longer view than private markets, they can stay active when private finance is in retreat—just as we have seen over the past two years.

Thus, under this complementary approach, it should be possible for public sector financial institutions both to improve the operation of financial markets (by filling gaps and meeting evolving market needs) and to avoid financial losses (by being smart when it comes to risk assessment and financial management).

With this concept in mind, the federal government has taken an evolutionary approach toward its financial Crown corporations since the mid-1990s. Each of the three federal financial institutions has carved out a quasi-commercial niche within its respective segment of the Canadian financial services industry—small and mid-sized business financing for BDC, facilitation of international trade and investment for EDC, and farms and agri-business credit for FCC. Each must maintain the balancing act of extending credit to meet public policy objectives within a commercial business mandate (i.e., generating profits). BDC and EDC, in particular, have expanded their roles as complementary players in their respective financial market segments. They are using a variety of financial instruments to take on credit risks alongside private sector lenders and insurers, thereby expanding the credit risk capacity of the entire Canadian financial system.

The three organizations have many supporters in the private business community, including in the financial services industry. But they also have critics who say these organizations are crowding out private credit activity; and some question whether these organizations should continue to exist at all.

RESPONDING TO THE FINANCIAL CRISIS

The financial crisis answered that question definitively. As the crisis began to choke off private credit to Canadian business (from Canadian and foreign sources) in the fall of 2008, the federal government quickly realized that it could use its own financial institutions—BDC and EDC in particular—to address specific financial market failures. The federal government chose to invest an additional $350 million in BDC's capital base in order to strengthen the bank's capacity to take risks and innovate during this challenging period. In addition to pursuing its regular lending and venture capital business, BDC created a new credit facility to purchase up to $12 billion of term asset-backed securities (ABS) backed by loans and leases on vehicles and equipment, reflecting the sharp decline in this particular market segment. Not surprisingly, BDC provided more financing in its business year ending March 31, 2010, than at any time in its history—$4.4 billion, or an increase of 53 per cent over the previous year,

For EDC, the federal government invested a similar amount—$350 million in new capital—to support up to $1.5 billion in increased credit capacity for those most affected by the financial crisis. EDC's mandate was also expanded for a two-year period to allow it to provide domestic financing and insurance for receivables. EDC facilitated Canadian international business to the tune of $82.8 billion in 2009, at a time when the risks associated with trade financing and insurance had increased around the globe and Canadian and global exports had dropped sharply.

Both BDC and EDC are working closely with private financial institutions to help build a bridge back to more normal credit conditions. The January 2009 federal budget included the creation of the Business Credit Availability Program (BCAP) to provide $5 billion in extra credit over two years. The BCAP is managed jointly by the private financial institutions, BDC, and EDC. Observers of the Canadian financial system have lauded this program as a major success.

It should also be noted that another federal institution, the Canada Mortgage and Housing Corporation, played a significant role in sustaining the Canadian mortgage market during the financial crisis.

For the foreseeable future, we expect the various public sector financial institutions covered in this chapter to continue to operate at a high level in terms of credit extended. Private capital markets have begun to heal, and private investment slowly began to grow again in 2010; but the global financial system is still a long way from normal. Financial markets are particularly worried about the financial condition of governments and banks in Europe. Significant gaps will continue to exist in specific financial markets, and the public sector institutions will have an ongoing role to play in bridging those gaps and encouraging a return to more normal risk-taking capacity for private lenders and insurers.

CONCLUSION

Public sector financial institutions internationally and in Canada have proven their collective value as policy tools for shoring up a severely weakened global financial system. The "Sleeping Beauty" or "state of readiness" strategy of public sector finance has worked. It was extremely useful—globally and within Canada—to have in place public sector institutions that could ramp up their operations when the private market failed. They will be needed as active financial players for some time to come, filling the gaps that widened in the financial marketplace.

LESSON 5

Global Coordination Was Critical to a Speedy Recovery

by *Glen Hodgson*

HIGHLIGHTS

- A key lesson from the Great Depression was that uncoordinated acts, such as competitive currency devaluation or protectionism, are ultimately self-defeating.
- Since the financial crisis struck, the G20 has done a number of things with remarkable speed.
- The crisis breathed new life into the important roles of the International Monetary Fund and World Bank, and catalyzed the formalization of the G20 group at the summit level.
- There is now a risk that financial stability and global economic growth will allow complacency to return and preclude further efforts to strengthen economic cooperation.

Today's global economy is deeply interconnected, and in times of economic crisis, global policy coordination is critical to a recovery. Coordination creates a shared responsibility, encourages the taking of bold action, increases the buy-in of all parties, and produces superior economic outcomes than do countries acting alone. The G20 has emerged from this crisis as the new driver of global economic cooperation, and of collective action and responsibility—if sufficient alignment can be maintained among its members.

WHY POLICY COORDINATION?

When an economic or financial crisis erupts and crosses international boundaries, national governments can respond in one of two ways: they can act separately, in what they believe to be their own best interests; or they can coordinate their response with other governments and take collective action. Given the magnitude and interconnectedness of the deep problems of late 2008 and much of 2009, it is not surprising that individual countries quickly recognized that acting alone would not be sufficient to deal with the financial crisis and resulting global recession. A coordinated global response, they quickly determined, offered the best hope of recovery.

Since the creation of the International Monetary Fund and the World Bank in 1944, governments have been developing institutions and processes through which they can take collective action to smooth out disruptions in the global economy.

That wasn't always the case. During the Great Depression of the 1930s, little effort was made to encourage economic policy cooperation or collective action among nations, even though the depression had spread across much of the world. Individual nations engaged in destructive acts. Some carried out competitive currency devaluations—a deliberate reduction in the international value of their currencies so as to make their goods cheaper (and thus more attractive) abroad, while at the same time raising the price of (and thus discouraging) imports. Some countries also erected barriers to international trade and investment via high tariffs and non-tariff barriers—again, in a misguided attempt to give local producers an advantage in their home markets.

A key lesson from the Great Depression is that protectionist reactions are ultimately self-defeating. The frustrating of international commerce, the taking of unilateral protectionist action, and the absence of policy consultation and coordination among nations all helped to fuel a global pullback in international trade and investment flows during the 1930s. Protectionism only served to create barriers for consumers while discouraging new productive investment and more efficient global production, thereby adding to the length, severity, and misery of the Depression.

CREATION OF INTERNATIONAL ECONOMIC INSTITUTIONS

A different philosophy emerged from the discussions among the Allies during the Second World War and the post-war period—one that favoured sustainable macroeconomic policies, free trade, and economic cooperation among nations. It was agreed that collective action by many nations was needed to diagnose, address, and solve economic and financial problems that could never be solved by one nation acting alone. Economic cooperation was seen as a three-legged stool made up of the IMF, the World Bank, and an international trade organization (that began life in 1947 as the General Agreement on Tariffs and Trade, or GATT, and was replaced in 1995 by the World Trade Organization, or WTO).

The IMF was created for another economic era—one of fixed exchange rates, pegged to gold. When the fixed exchange rate system began to collapse in the early 1970s, the IMF had to find a way to evolve or risk becoming irrelevant. Fortunately, the IMF was also given a mandate at the outset to assess the adequacy and appropriateness of each member country's economic policies, particularly macroeconomic policies, and to provide credit to countries with financing needs. By refocusing its efforts around that core mandate, the IMF has managed to remain relevant, even as the global exchange rate and monetary system has changed so dramatically over the past four decades.

> **What was it about this most recent recession that made international cooperation so critical?**

For its part, the World Bank was given the task of providing capital for economic development and investment. Its initial lending in the post-war period was aimed at promoting stabilization and recovery in the war-ravaged countries of Europe and Asia. Later, its operations were expanded, making it a principal source of investment capital throughout the developing world. And while the growth of private capital markets over the past two decades caused the World Bank's role to shrink in many borrowing countries, the Bank continues to be a significant player globally, particularly in lower-income developing nations.

As for the pursuit of freer international trade, the initial plan was to launch an International Trade Organization (ITO) as the third leg of the global coordination stool. The ITO would champion free trade and work to reduce global trade barriers. However, opposition within the U.S. Congress blocked U.S. ratification of the ITO charter—and without the United States on board, there could be no ITO. The General Agreement on Tariffs and Trade, therefore, emerged as the best alternative for the pursuit of free trade. The GATT was an agreement among signatories, not a formal trade institution, and was enhanced and strengthened through successive free trade negotiating rounds. It wasn't until January 1, 1995, that the institutional form of a global advocate for free trade—the World Trade Organization—finally emerged.

The WTO continues to push actively for global free trade, despite the frustration of the stalled Doha round (2001–) of negotiations. (Failure to agree on more open trade in agricultural products is one major stumbling block.) To try to build a commitment to free trade, the WTO also assesses the trade policies of its members.

Over the last seven decades, global financial and economic cooperation has evolved and expanded. The global framework has included forums for discussions among central banks (such as the Bank for International Settlements, often referred to as "a bank for central banks"), various regional development banks, think-tanks such as the Organisation for Economic Co-operation and Development, and the various groupings of nations that consult regularly—such as the G7, G8, G10, G22, G24, and G77. Occasionally, these groupings have worked together toward a common goal. More often, there has been conflict between the clubs representing the interests of the rich countries (such as the G7) and those that are dominated by developing countries (such as the G24 or G77).

THE RISE OF THE G20

What was it about this most recent recession that made international cooperation so critical? The answer is the massive scale and scope of the financial crisis, which this time transcended the G7 to include virtually the entire world economy. The financial systems of many industrial countries were severely weakened by the crisis—the G7 alone could not solve the problem. It helped that political pressure had already been growing to expand the club of leading nations, driven by the ongoing shift in economic power toward emerging nations, such as China, India, and Brazil. As well, it had become abundantly clear that one of the key reasons for the crisis was the significant imbalance in savings and investment between key developed and developing countries—with China a key source of global savings, and the U.S. a significant net borrower of those funds.

> **In terms of fiscal stimulus, it was actually the IMF that recommended a target of 2 per cent of GDP.**

Fortunately, the core for a wider club of leading nations than the G7 already existed. Finance ministers and central bank governors from 19 influential nations plus the European Union first met in Berlin in 1999 to launch the G20. (Canada's finance minister at the time, Paul Martin, was a key figure in the creation of the G20.) When the global financial crisis struck, it acted as a catalyst for bringing the G20 up to the summit level. The first summit meeting was held in Washington in November 2008 and brought together the leaders of the 19 member nations, the EU, plus the IMF and the World Bank to discuss options for addressing the financial crisis and recession.[1]

---

1   The G20 members are Argentina, Australia, Brazil, Canada, China, France, Germany, India, Indonesia, Italy, Japan, Mexico, Russia, Saudi Arabia, South Africa, South Korea, Turkey, the United Kingdom, the United States, plus the presidency of the European Union. The IMF and World Bank are also *de facto* members.

There is some irony in the fact that the initial G20 summit in November 2008 was called by the administration of U.S. President George W. Bush—hardly a champion of internationalism. However, the Bush White House recognized the importance of including all countries and regions that play significant roles in the international financial system; and it also understood the limitations of the G7 in dealing with a financial crisis of this magnitude. Washington believed that the financial and leadership capacity of the U.S. or the G7 alone would not be sufficient to deal with the financial crisis. The crisis posed a risk, not just to U.S. banks, consumers, and businesses, but to the entire global financial and economic system. Collective action of a truly global scale—via the G20—was therefore needed to resolve a financial crisis that had quickly become global in nature.

What has the G20 actually accomplished in its three summit meetings so far? Since the financial crisis struck, it has done a number of things with remarkable speed. The G20 started by creating a broad and inclusive platform for collective action. In practical terms, that meant creating a network of officials from national governments and their central banks—people who could discuss and negotiate on what the financial stabilization and economic recovery plan should look like. (Like a duck paddling around a pond, much of the effort that propels the G20 forward is hidden below the surface away from public view, which may contribute to an under-appreciation of how much work is actually taking place.)

The G20 next established common principles for financial sector reform. The leaders' statement issued at the close of their November 2008 summit set out (after much heated debate) principles recognizing that responsibility for strengthened financial sector regulation rests with the national authorities. But the principles also recognized the need for intensified international consultations among regulators and for more common international standards.

The next phase was to create greater alignment around the need for economic stimulus. Central bank monetary authorities, who are in regular contact with each other, had already intervened in their national financial markets. They were slashing interest rates and even considering quantitative easing to avoid deflation and kindle the recovery. In terms of fiscal stimulus, it was actually the IMF that recommended a target of 2 per cent of GDP, which became the accepted global standard.

The second G20 summit was held in London in April 2009. There, the G20 advanced the agenda further by forming a consensus and work plan for enhanced collective action on financing for countries in crisis, through the IMF, World Bank, and the regional development banks. The leaders agreed to:

- triple the resources available to the IMF—to $750 billion;
- support a new special drawing rights (SDR) allocation by the IMF of $250 billion;
- support new lending by the global development banks of at least $100 billion;
- provide $250 billion in financing to support global trade; and
- sell IMF gold, with the proceeds to be used to provide financial help to the poorest countries.

Together, the announced financing package added up to more than $1 trillion in collective global action.

By the time of the third G20 summit in Pittsburgh in September 2009, the tone had changed from one of halting the damage to one of building for recovery. The summit communiqué talked of the need to lay a foundation for concerted action. At the same time, the leaders recognized the power shift in the global economy, as they agreed to a redistribution of quota shares at the IMF, giving the emerging economic powers a greater voice.

The fourth meeting of the G20 took place in June 2010 in Toronto. While much of the media focus was on the turmoil in the streets outside, the meeting produced a high degree of alignment (if not unanimity) on the need to begin reducing fiscal deficits and restoring investor confidence. However, it did not make similar progress in building a consensus on financial sector regulatory reform. That issue was left for other forums in the hope that an agreement would be completed by the next meeting in South Korea in November 2010.

One area in which G20 announcements to date ring a bit hollow is their commitment to free trade and resistance to protectionism. As the Brookings Institution and Global Trade Alert noted, many G20 members, despite voicing their commitment to resisting protectionism, introduced new trade barriers—some subtle, some obvious—in response to the crisis and recession. Moreover, although the G20 vowed to do what it can to complete the Doha round of global trade talks by the end of 2010, there was little sign of progress—leading some observers, such as *The Economist*, to describe the G20 pledge as "weak and implausible."

Similarly, the G20's commitment to ongoing climate change negotiations is a wild card. The 2009 Copenhagen negotiations on climate change ended in a stalemate over several key issues, and the next steps in the process are murky at best. Power and influence has clearly shifted away from Europe, which had been the driving force, and toward emerging market nations where greenhouse gas emissions are growing rapidly. These nations' dialogue with the United States will define the shape of future climate change negotiations.

WHAT NEXT FOR THE G20?

The G20 calendar is full and complex. The groups' governance structure has been complicated by Canada and South Korea acting as co-hosts in 2010—Canada hosted the summit in late June in Toronto, while the job of hosting the November meeting went to South Korea. The running agenda is no less complicated, with seemingly perpetual discussions on issues ranging from financial sector regulatory reform to designing strategies for governments to exit the exceptional bout of economic stimulus.

The sustainability of the G20 will be put to the test as the impact of the stimulus wanes and each country charts its own course for restoring more normal monetary and fiscal conditions. Although global economic growth has returned, financial risks continue to spook financial markets. Unemployment is high and declining only slowly in many countries, and growth in private investment has also been slow to recover. A second round of stimulus remains a possibility—albeit, a shrinking possibility—

in some G20 countries (notably the U.S.), but is unlikely in most cases. Indeed, the fiscal cost of stimulus has quickly become a significant issue, making an approach to steady fiscal adjustment based on cooperation even more critical.

> **There are growing differences among G20 members on the extent of financial regulatory reforms deemed necessary.**

In many countries, substantive financial sector reform has been slow to take shape. The G20 will have an important role in assessing progress on this front, not only in holding countries accountable for action on financial reform implementation, but also in determining the right degree of financial sector reform. Already, there are growing differences among G20 members on the extent of financial regulatory reforms deemed necessary, and this may remain a continuing point of friction.

Lastly, exchange rate policy—in particular, the alignment of exchange rates among major currencies—has flared up as a hot issue. U.S. and other leaders have accused China of seeking a competitive advantage by keeping the yuan at a deflated value against the U.S. dollar. Other major currencies—such as the euro, yen, and British pound—are seeking out their fundamental value, with occasional and, at times, questionable government intervention. Whether and how exchange rates will be allowed to find their market-clearing (or equilibrium) levels could be an ongoing source of irritation within the G20.

CONCLUSION

The financial crisis and resulting recession gave new impetus to the need for economic cooperation among nations. The crisis breathed fresh life into the important roles of the IMF and World Bank, and catalyzed the formalization of the G20 group at the summit level. A steady shift in global economic power was already taking place in favour of emerging nations, such as China, India, and Brazil; and the financial crisis further eroded the financial capacity and political legitimacy of the G7.

The G20 has emerged as the new driver of global economic cooperation, and of collective action and responsibility. This is an important development since it reflects the ongoing shift in global economic and political power. The challenge will be to keep building the effectiveness and credibility of the G20 as an institution, and to rebalance the governance of the IMF, World Bank, and other organizations to reflect the new geopolitical reality without undermining their capacity to provide solid policy advice and financial support.

As we witnessed during the global recession of 2008–09, global economic cooperation occurs most actively during times of crisis. Today, there is a risk that financial stability and global economic growth will allow complacency to return and preclude further efforts to strengthen economic cooperation. Even modest sustained global growth could relieve the policy pressure and permit a drift back to uncoordinated policies and practices. Despite the many lessons from the financial crisis and recession, the world might well tacitly accept that sustained but weaker global aggregate demand is "normal."

LESSON 6

"Too Big to Fail" Means Too Big

by *Michael Burt*

HIGHLIGHTS

- During the recession, governments bailed out several financial and industrial giants because they were deemed to be "too big to fail."
- Canada generally resisted the urge to directly provide public assistance to ailing companies, with one major exception—the automakers.
- Given the fiscal burden imposed on governments by the rescuing of firms that were "too big to fail," there is a valid public policy rationale for minimizing the risks that those organizations pose to a country and its economy.

How the mighty have fallen. The list of corporate titans that turned to governments for various forms of assistance during the financial crisis is both long and impressive. While financial institutions were the main beneficiaries of government aid, industrial giants—such as GM and Chrysler—also asked for, and received, government assistance. The common justification for handing out this largesse was that these firms were "too big to fail."

WHAT DOES "TOO BIG TO FAIL" MEAN?

Business failures are a part of everyday life. According to Statistics Canada data, only about one in five businesses survive their first ten years, with tens of thousands of businesses being born and dying every year. During times of economic weakness, business death rates increase and birth rates slow. The result is a net decline in job creation and business activity. This is the process that renowned economist Joseph Schumpeter (1883–1950) referred to as "creative destruction," whereby labour and capital are continually being reapplied to new ideas in the never-ending quest to increase productivity and provide goods and services at a lower price. Firms rise and fall as part of the rhythm of creative destruction.

So, when so many firms are simply allowed to fail, what makes a select few special enough to receive assistance? The answer is that the failure of these few could pose a systemic risk to the operation of the economy—either by causing severe damage to the financial system, a particular market, or the entire economy. This fear is driven by the idea that every organization has linkages with others, and the collapse of one of the giants can lead to the subsequent collapse of other smaller firms that are otherwise healthy. This can happen through real transactional linkages or reputational effects. In the world of finance, for example, a run on a bank can lead to the failure of that institution, which in turn can lead to a loss of confidence in others. An example outside the world of finance was the demise of the accounting firm Arthur Andersen after its reputation as an auditor was tarnished by the 2001 collapse of Enron.

In practical terms, the most likely arguments for why a firm poses a systematic risk are that the firm employs a large number of people, either directly or through its linkages to the rest of the economy; the firm has a large market share; or some combination of the two.

If a company employs a million people, or if it is the dominant provider of a product or service—particularly one that is critical to the operation of the economy (such as financial services)—a case could be made that the company's failure poses a systemic risk to the operation of the country's economy. The first argument—that too many jobs would be lost—is the one the automakers employed. The second argument—that their services are critically important to the economy—is the key reason why Fannie Mae, Freddie Mac, and AIG are all now essentially owned by the U.S. government.

These arguments are open to debate. Wal-Mart is the largest employer in North America. Does that mean that if Wal-Mart were in danger of failing, it should get assistance from the government? Microsoft's global market share for personal computer operating systems is nearly 90 per cent.[1] Would it qualify? In reality, a firm that declares bankruptcy does not necessarily disappear, and demand for its products definitely does not. In general, consumers of those products will simply choose a different vendor, or continue to be served by a firm as it goes through bankruptcy restructuring. Wal-Mart's competitors would be eager to gobble up its market share if it ever went bankrupt.

Overly large firms may pose a systemic risk to the operation of the economy—either by causing severe damage to the financial system, a particular market, or the entire economy.

The automakers augmented their case by including parts manufacturers, wholesalers, and retailers in their employment statistics. The assumption was that nearly all those businesses would be shuttered in the event of the failure of GM or Chrysler—thus creating a systemic risk. However, since people would continue to buy vehicles by simply substituting to different brands, at least a portion of the related supply chain would be reallocated to the remaining players. Dealers would switch to selling different brands of cars, and parts suppliers would switch to other automakers, expecting that demand for the remaining brands would increase.

During the recent recession, Canada generally resisted the urge to directly provide public assistance to ailing companies. Automakers were the major exception. In the case of GM and Chrysler, the policy decisions were driven by the high degree of integration in the North American auto industry and by the U.S. government's determination to

---

1   See StatOwl.com, "Operating Systems Market Share." Stat Owl. www.statowl.com/operating_system_market_share.php (accessed September 10, 2010).

provide assistance. If Canada had not proportionately matched the assistance that the U.S. government was providing, we would very likely have seen the end of Chrysler and GM's presence in Canada.

The relative health of our financial institutions is a key reason why Canada was generally able to resist the call for bailouts. Our ability to extend credit to firms during the crisis through existing financial Crown corporations—such as the Business Development Bank of Canada and Export Development Canada—also helped.[2]

THE CONSEQUENCES OF BEING TOO BIG

If we accept that firms can indeed be "too big to fail" under certain circumstances, the next question is whether it is desirable for these firms to exist at that scale. The short answer is no. Under the current system, in which there is no explicit definition of systemic risk, large organizations are *de facto* free to take risks and reap any rewards, while passing on the risk of business-ending activities to taxpayers. This mismatch between risk and reward encourages organizations to take unnecessary risks and may lead to poor business decisions. The problem is generally referred to as "moral hazard" and is often used in the context of the insurance industry. Essentially, when someone is protected from the consequences of certain risks, their behaviour regarding those risks may change.

Perhaps the most egregious example of this imbalance between risk and reward was the case of Freddie Mac and Fannie Mae in the United States. Both organizations were government-sponsored enterprises (GSEs) created by the federal government and given a mandate to improve access to mortgage credit. However, they were also publicly traded companies. As a result of this unusual arrangement, they received an implicit guarantee. The market behaved as though Fannie Mae and Freddie Mac were backstopped by the U.S. federal government, and they were thus able to borrow funds at effectively the same rate as the federal government—well below the market rates for even the highest-rated

---

2   See "Lesson 4: Public Sector Financial Institutions Prove Their Worth."

for-profit businesses. This implicit subsidy led the two firms to become the dominant buyers of mortgages in the secondary market. Their combined market share seldom fell below half, and for extended periods surpassed 70 per cent.

> **The implicit guarantee that comes from "too big to fail" status creates "moral hazard"—when an organization is protected from the consequences of certain risks, its behaviour regarding these risks may change.**

The risks embedded in this combination of private ownership and implicit public guarantee were well documented and debated in the years leading up to the housing bust. These concerns did lead to Fannie Mae and Freddie Mac being restricted as to what types of mortgages they could buy, thus limiting their exposure to many of the exotic and subprime mortgages that contributed to the housing bust. However, these restrictions were not enough to prevent them from falling into financial crisis and having to be nationalized—which is exactly what happened at the height of the bust. Indeed, their narrow mandate may have contributed to their eventual downfall, since they were restricted from investing in non-mortgage-related securities.

The result was that, for years, shareholders enjoyed the benefit of an implicit subsidy, while taxpayers were ultimately on the hook for the mistakes that these firms made. Thanks to the implicit guarantee, the firms were able to become dominant players in the U.S. residential mortgage market. And as a result of their integral importance to the residential mortgage market, once they were on the verge of failure, the government was forced to act in order to prevent this critical financial market segment from seizing up completely. The implicit guarantee became explicit.

Concern over the creation of moral hazard was a major reason why investment banking giant Lehman Brothers was allowed to fail in September of 2008. By that point, however, markets already believed Lehman enjoyed an implicit guarantee. Six months earlier, the U.S.

Federal Reserve had orchestrated the buyout of Bear Stearns, the smallest of the "big five" investment banks, over concerns that its collapse might pose a systemic risk. Thus, as the larger Merrill Lynch and Lehman Brothers faced increasing pressure late in the summer of 2008, bailouts or shotgun marriages were expected for them as well. While Merrill Lynch was eventually purchased by Bank of America, no lifeline for Lehman Brothers appeared. In the days following its collapse, credit markets virtually shut down and the stock market plunged—largely because U.S. policy-makers did not carry through on the implicit guarantee.

THE CURE

While the government guarantee of other large organizations may be more tenuous than it was for the GSEs, any belief among senior managers that they are "too big to fail" could contribute to unnecessary risk taking or, conversely, a sense of complacency that leads to insufficient risk management. Better forms of regulation are the key to resolving this market failure. The objective would be to prevent firms from getting so big that their failure threatens a country's economy. Or if their size is deemed desirable due to economies of scale, then their risk-taking behaviour should be limited.

Enhanced competition laws are one possible means to this end. As firms become dominant in their market, they often become subject to anti-trust scrutiny. However, at present, the focus of competition rules is the protection of competition in general and consumers in particular. There is no consideration of the implications for the economy, or for government fiscal liabilities, of having very large firms. If systemic risk is to be taken into account, countries would have to consider additional criteria when assessing competition laws or undertaking competition studies (such as on whether proposed mergers would create systemic risks for an economy and for government).

To be truly effective, these considerations would have to extend beyond proposed mergers to address firms that may already be "too big" or that grow to become too big organically. As such, regulatory standards would need to be established to assess systemic risk based on firm size and interconnectedness. Once certain triggers were met, governments would have to decide if an organization should be broken up to reduce systemic risk. Possible triggers could include a firm's direct and indirect share of national employment, its market share, and the size of its contribution to the country's fiscal purse.

Although it has a variety of potential problems, breaking up "too large" firms is one potential policy response.

We recognize that this approach poses several potential problems. For example, this system could discourage businesses approaching the triggers for a formal review from wanting to keep growing. This could push new business growth offshore and into other jurisdictions. There is also the important question of how the triggers would be set. The triggers would need to vary by jurisdiction, potentially leading to large multinational companies shopping around for the best spot to set up their operations and possibly preventing their development in smaller countries. Finally, there is no guarantee that several smaller firms will behave differently than one large one. In essence, several smaller firms may inadvertently expose themselves to the same risk.

These potential problems may limit the practical application of breakups as a policy tool, but breaking up larger firms may sometimes be the appropriate public policy response. Though such a solution may appear extreme, it has been done in the past to improve competitive forces for a particular product. (The court-ordered 1984 breakup of AT&T is the most prominent example.) As well, to maintain competition, governments often require companies during the merger and acquisition approval process to divest certain assets.

It is important to remember that firms already restructure themselves. Stock markets often under-value the stocks of conglomerates because it is difficult to manage large businesses with disparate products. This response from financial markets can persuade companies to divest themselves of businesses unrelated to their core products, or to split along divisional lines. Recent examples include Genworth Financial splitting from General Electric; Kraft being spun off from Altria; and in Canada, EnCana's divestiture of its oil sands business, which became Cenovus Energy.

Instituting risk-control measures, such as capital requirements for banks, would help prevent the outright failure of "too large" firms under foreseeable circumstances.

Sometimes, the nature of a particular business requires an organization to be a certain size and/or have a certain market share to operate effectively and efficiently. One reason why there are relatively few vehicle manufacturers around the world is that auto making is a capital-intensive business requiring considerable investments in supply chains, marketing, and engineering. Thus, a company needs a minimum level of sales to be able to provide a competitive product at a price that most consumers can afford.

In such cases, limiting the size of a firm would not necessarily be desirable or possible. Instead, restrictions on the risks that it can take could be defined and put into place—restrictions sufficient to prevent the outright failure of that organization under foreseeable circumstances. The risk requirements would need to vary, depending on the nature of a particular business, but they would be similar in design and motivation to capital requirements for banks.

Although complicated to design and implement, and likely to face considerable resistance from the businesses to be regulated, increased oversight would be necessary if systemic risk is to be reduced. Still, it is possible that a firm deemed to be "too big to fail" could indeed fail due to unforeseen circumstances or complacency. It was not excessive risk taking, but a host of long-term structural problems, coupled with the recession, that brought about GM's bankruptcy.

As such, a final piece of public policy may be needed to solve the "too big to fail" problem. Essentially, if a firm posing a systemic risk is allowed to continue operating as is, a contingency plan could be established to deal with its unanticipated failure. At a minimum, creating a type of "living will" would allow some consistency in policy, preventing solutions from being devised on the fly at a time of stress, which is a recipe for making poor decisions. It would also allow stakeholders to understand what they could lose in the event of failure, thus giving them an incentive to cooperate with regulators to reduce that possibility.

At a minimum, the creation of "living wills" for "too big to fail" firms would allow for some consistency in policy and allow stakeholders to understand what they could lose in the event of a failure.

ADVANCING THE AGENDA

In the wake of the global financial crisis, various governments are now seeking a means to address the "too big to fail" problem. The Dodd-Frank Act, which became law in the United States in July 2010, is one such effort. This ambitious reform of financial regulation tackled a wide array of issues. Dodd-Frank established clear lines of responsibility for regulators, increased oversight and disclosure rules for a variety of financial products and firms (including over-the-counter derivatives and hedge funds), and introduced regulations aimed at reducing conflicts of interest and increasing transparency at credit rating agencies.

The Act also created the Financial Stability Oversight Council, chaired by the Treasury Secretary. Council members consist of representatives from the different federal financial regulators, including the Federal Reserve Board and the Securities and Exchange Commission. Its purpose is to monitor, assess, and mitigate systemic risk to the U.S. financial system. The council has been given considerable powers to meet this goal. For example, it will limit the proprietary trading activity of banks and non-banks. The council can also discourage excessive growth and complexity by setting rules for capital requirements, leverage, liquidity, and risk management that increase as companies grow. As a last resort, the council can even require a "too large" firm to divest some of its holdings if that firm is deemed to pose a "grave threat" to the financial stability of the United States.

The council has also been given the power to extend the reach of regulators beyond the traditional banking sector. For example, the council can apply the regulatory requirements for banks to non-bank financial firms, such as insurance companies, if they are deemed to be a systemic risk. As well, oversight of systemically important clearing, payments, and settlements systems has been clearly identified as being under the purview of the Federal Reserve Board.

Finally, since failures may still occur despite this increase in regulation, large and complex companies will be required to periodically submit plans for their orderly shutdown and liquidation in the event of failure. In essence, companies will be required to file and regularly update a "living will." It is expected that the requirement to produce a plan deemed credible by regulators will limit the interest of financial firms in products and services that cannot be easily unwound. There is also a provision in the Act that requires surviving financial firms to pay back any government funds that are used in the process of unwinding a failed company. It is expected that this provision will give leverage to regulators when organizing private rescues, which are generally preferable to liquidations.

In short, the Dodd-Frank Act encapsulates all three of the policy recommendations outlined above: living wills, increased regulatory oversight, and—as a last resort—breaking up companies that are too large. One thing that it does not do is address the potential problem of non-financial firms that may be "too big to fail." It is true that systemic risk is usually discussed in the context of the financial system due to its interconnectedness with every other part of the economy and the fact that confidence is critical to its proper functioning.[3] However, the U.S. and Canadian governments did extend assistance to GM and Chrysler at the height of the recession under the rationale that they were "too big to fail."

---

3   See "Lesson 3: The Financial Sector Is Unique and Needs New Standards."

If these giant companies are indeed too big to be allowed to go under, then the objectives of the Financial Stability Oversight Council should be extended beyond the financial services sector.

It is also important to note that although these steps have been taken in the United States, there has been little impetus to assess or mitigate systemic risks in Canada. Because Canada did not experience a financial crisis of its own, this has not been a major topic of discussion among policy-makers. Although better regulation in Canada did limit the damage to the Canadian economy caused by the global financial crisis, this does not mean that systemic risks cannot arise here. As such, it would be better to act to identify and control those risks now, before a crisis occurs.

CONCLUSION

Business failures are common—indeed, they are generally healthy, since they allow limited financial and labour resources to be redeployed to better uses. In some circumstances, however, the costs of a particular firm's failure may be catastrophic to an economy as a whole; in essence, the firm is "too big to fail." In such cases, it is in the public interest to limit the systemic risk. It is far better to actively manage the risks associated with a "too big" firm than to try to orchestrate an expensive rescue plan at the height of a crisis.

The costs related to the failure of large institutions can be catastrophic. Smaller countries are particularly vulnerable, since they cannot cover the liabilities of their large businesses. National bankruptcy and economic collapse can be the result—as was the case in Iceland. Therefore, if businesses truly are "too big to fail," then the state has a responsibility to effectively take out an insurance policy—in the form of increased regulatory oversight—against catastrophic failure.

The first step in creating such an insurance policy is to define the parameters of what poses a systemic risk to the country. Measures such as a firm's direct and indirect share of national employment, its market share, and the size of its contribution to the country's fiscal purse should be considered. Although these parameters would vary by country (depending on such factors as the country's industry mix and the size of its economy), international coordination would be desirable to avoid reducing the competitiveness of the country's firms.

Once a list of firms posing potential systemic risks is drawn up, regulators would next have to determine how those risks could be reduced or even eliminated. At a minimum, the creation of living wills would detail ahead of time the steps to be taken in the event of a business failure. We expect that the risks associated with moral hazard would be reduced if the cost of failure were explicitly laid out to stakeholders.

A more comprehensive regulatory regime may also be needed. This would require designing industry-specific risk measures, similar in motivation to capital requirements for banks or covenants on debt. The purpose would be to prevent the failure of an organization under foreseeable circumstances. Finally, the most invasive step would be to break up firms deemed "too big to fail." This may not be practicable in many circumstances, but it is a policy option that regulators have used in the past for other reasons (as they did in the 1984 breakup of AT&T).

The Financial Stability Oversight Council created under the Dodd-Frank Act in the United States incorporates all three of these policy options: living wills, increased regulatory oversight, and, potentially, breakups. However, Canada has yet to formally recognize or address the potential costs imposed by systemic risks.

Minimizing the regulatory burden on businesses is generally advisable. However, the financial and economic events of 2008 and 2009 suggest that the status quo is not sufficient. Given the fiscal burden imposed on governments by the rescue of firms that were deemed "too big to fail," there is a real public policy rationale for minimizing the risks that these businesses pose to a country and its economy.

LESSON 7

Integrative Trade Can Pull Us Down and Back Up

by *Danielle Goldfarb*

> **HIGHLIGHTS**
>
> - The collapse of international trade and global supply chains—or "integrative trade"—likely pulled us more deeply into recession than would otherwise have been the case.
> - While protectionism rose in the wake of the recession, deep global linkages may have limited its reach.
> - Expanded "integrative trade" can help drive the recovery and beyond, providing that policy-makers resist protectionist impulses and adopt policies in line with the realities of today's globally integrated production.

One lesson from the recession and financial crisis is that international trade helped pull Canada and the world into recession. At the same time, deep global linkages—or "integrative trade"—may have helped to blunt the protectionist response and can help to better position the Canadian and global economies coming out of the global slowdown and beyond.

STEEP TRADE DECLINE DRIVEN BY INTEGRATIVE TRADE

Over the past several decades, global trade exploded, but it plummeted at the end of 2008 and in 2009. Behind both this explosion and sudden retrenchment of trade is "integrative trade"—the use of global and regional supply chains. In recent years, businesses have accelerated their sourcing of parts and services from all over the world. So when global demand fell sharply, trade fell even more sharply as businesses pulled back on their international supply chains. This is consistent with past recessions and slowdowns—during the down cycles, trade in intermediate inputs typically declines.[1]

Global trade volumes fell by almost 11 per cent in 2009, according to the International Monetary Fund.[2] Developed economies saw their exports and their imports fall—on average, by 12 per cent each. For the developing economies, that number was roughly 8 per cent.[3] Canada's exports and imports also dropped steeply and in parallel with each other. Canada's heavy integration into U.S. supply chains meant that when U.S. demand collapsed, Canadian–U.S. supply chains took a hard hit. Canadian merchandise export and import volumes both fell 15 per cent in 2009.

INTEGRATIVE TRADE CAN PULL US BACK UP

The balance of evidence shows that international trade, including the use of global and regional supply chains, boosts living standards over the longer term. Growth in "integrative trade" is likely to be a key driver of the global economy in the future.

Indeed, the global and Canadian economies saw robust trade growth in 2010. The IMF predicted global trade growth of 11 per cent in 2010 and 7 per cent in 2011, driven mostly by the developing economies.[4] For Canada, The Conference Board of Canada estimated that export volumes will grow by 7 per cent in both 2010 and 2011, and that imports will grow by 9 per cent in 2010 and 7 per cent in 2011.

While the growing reliance on global and regional supply chains was a factor in the downturn, it is also likely to drive future trade growth. Intermediate goods trade—an indicator of global supply chain activity—

---

1   Sturgeon and Memedovic, *Looking for Global Value Chains.*

2   International Monetary Fund, *World Economic Outlook.*

3   Ibid.

4   Ibid.

tends to rebound strongly after down cycles. This was true, for example, following the 1997 East Asian financial crisis. A key reason for the rebound in intermediate goods trade is that when expansion resumes, companies are more likely to outsource production—often offshore—rather than invest in internal capacity, since they still face uncertain demand.[5]

> **While the growing reliance on global and regional supply chains was a factor in the economic downturn, it is also likely to drive future trade growth.**

A similar response is likely this time around—unless businesses fail to take advantage of emerging opportunities, or policy-makers stand in the way.

THE THREAT OF NEW TRADE BARRIERS

History warns us of the consequences of erecting new trade barriers. As many have noted, the U.S. government responded to the 1929 financial crisis by passing the Smoot-Hawley *Tariff Act of 1930*, which raised U.S. tariffs. The United States' trading partners quickly retaliated. Canada, for example, raised tariffs on imported U.S. products. As a result, U.S. trade was cut in half, exacerbating the Great Depression.

New trade barriers represent an even greater threat today, given the rise of integrative trade. Research In Motion's BlackBerry provides an example of how disruptive new barriers would be. The BlackBerry is produced in many locations and encounters multiple borders. Component parts come from Asia, Europe, and the United States. The device is manufactured in Hungary and Mexico. Research and development and global after-sales service are based in Canada, and the units are sold around the world. The same is true for other electronics and products, such as cars and airplanes, that draw on regional and global supply chains. Any new

---

5   Sturgeon and Memedovic, *Looking for Global Value Chains.*

trade barriers will not only reduce the flow of final goods exports, but will have a domino effect on all of the related intermediate inputs. Worse, trade barriers could also start a tit-for-tat trade war—magnifying and widening the spread of the trade decline.

> **During the financial crisis, global leaders—especially G20 leaders—went out of their way to promise repeatedly that they would not revert to protectionism.**

Global leaders—especially G20 leaders—promised repeatedly that they would not revert to protectionism during the crisis. But when faced with the political realities of the recession, many broke their promise. We then saw such actions as the "Buy American" provisions in the U.S. stimulus bill, similar "Buy China" provisions launched by Beijing, and the U.S. decision to slap duties on Chinese tires.

Global Trade Alert (an independent organization that monitors global trade protectionism) found that between November 2008 and May 2010, governments put in place at least 400 measures that discriminate against foreign commercial interests.[6] As well, anti-dumping and other safeguard measures increased by over one-third in the first half of 2009 relative to the same period one year earlier, according to a study of the World Bank's Global Antidumping Database.[7]

While the direct effects of each measure may be relatively confined, the concern is the measures could lead to similar practices elsewhere, and could potentially escalate into a trade war. As experience has shown, this would likely destroy jobs, rather than protect them. The Peterson Institute for International Economics in Washington, D.C., for example, warns that "Buy American" could ultimately cost U.S. jobs if other countries adopt similarly protectionist policies.[8]

---

6   Evenett, *Africa Resists the Protectionist Temptation.*

7   Bown, *Protectionism Continues Its Climb.*

8   Hufbauer and Schott, *Buy American.*

DID INTEGRATIVE TRADE MITIGATE THE PROTECTIONIST RESPONSE?

While protectionism is clearly on the rise, things could have been worse. We did not see a repeat of across-the-board, 1930s-style protectionism. Global Trade Alert found that only five jurisdictions took measures that affected more than one-third of all product categories.[9] Protectionist measures introduced in the wake of the recession were likely to affect, at most, one-half of 1 per cent of world imports, according to the World Trade Organization (WTO).[10] And the World Bank found that protectionist measures, such as tariff increases or anti-dumping duties, accounted for less than 2 per cent of the collapse in world trade.[11] Moreover, by May 2010, the WTO found that announcements of new trade-restricting measures had slowed.[12]

> **New trade barriers represent an even greater threat today, given the rise of integrative trade.**

A recent article in the daily online magazine *The Globalist* described protectionism this time around as "the dog that did not bark."[13] Why did we not see an even more protectionist response? A key factor could be the acceleration of tight global linkages, which now make it less attractive to take protectionist actions. As the cost of coordinating among a range of global players globally has come down, the building of global supply chains has accelerated, and multinational companies are locating or outsourcing tasks to where they can be done most efficiently.

---

9   Evenett, *Africa Resists the Protectionist Temptation.*

10 World Trade Organization, *Report to the TPRB.*

11 Kee, Neagu, and Nicita, *Is Protectionism on the Rise?*

12 Ibid.

13 Alden, "Protectionism—The Dog That Didn't Bark."

Protectionism makes no sense in this context, and multinationals have a strong incentive to oppose it. Another contributing factor could be the role of WTO rules that limit the scope for protectionism.[14]

> According to the WTO, new protectionist measures could affect at most one-half of 1 per cent of world imports.

In short, tight global linkages may have blunted the protectionist response. Integrative trade may have made it easier for the world to learn the lesson of history that protectionist actions—such as the Smoot-Hawley tariffs—make a bad situation much worse.

Despite integrative trade's possible mitigating effect on protectionism, we cannot be complacent. The WTO notes that there is significant slack in the global economy—and if unemployment remains high, protectionism may intensify.[15] Global Trade Alert continued to report new protectionist actions in 2010.[16] There is still a significant risk that such actions could slow, or even derail, the global recovery and future economic growth.

GOING ON THE OFFENCE

In contrast to the country's actions in the 1930s, Canada was relatively well behaved this time around, resisting the temptation to erect new barriers. As well, Canada's tariffs are, on average, relatively low. But this is not only about defence. The global economy is highly competitive, as companies scramble to regain their previous economic footing. To seize global opportunities in this tough environment, Canada needs to use every available policy and business strategy tool.

---

14 Alden, "Protectionism—The Dog That Didn't Bark."

15 World Trade Organization, *Trade to Expand.*

16 Evenett, *Africa Resists the Protectionist Temptation.*

To Canada's credit, federal budgets in 2009 and 2010 removed tariffs on machinery and equipment. Ottawa managed to convince the provinces to offer U.S. businesses access to provincial procurement in exchange for exemptions from the "Buy American" provisions (though it is not clear how much damage had already been done). Canada also committed to negotiate a long-term agreement with the U.S. to gain access to each other's government procurement markets. However, Canada still has several tariff and non-tariff barriers that reduce Canadian company competitiveness and thwart its global ambitions over the long term. One notable example is the 200 to 300 per cent duties on most dairy products—duties that hamper the competitiveness of food processors. Other examples are local content provisions, such as those in Ontario's green energy program (which are being challenged under WTO rules).

Canada still has several tariff and non-tariff barriers that reduce Canadian company competitiveness and thwart its global ambitions over the long term.

Canadian policy-makers face a tremendous and ongoing challenge—maintaining and enhancing access to the U.S. market in the face of protectionist rhetoric and action. Achieving this goal is critical, but will not be easy. Smart Canadian policy-makers will also realize that the U.S. market could take some time to recover fully, and markets elsewhere offer tremendous opportunities. As the global economy recovers, policy-makers need to ensure Canada has access to markets beyond the United States. They should work to remove barriers that hinder Canadian companies from accessing large developing markets in Asia—markets that were growing rapidly before the recession and are likely to continue to experience rapid growth.

As well, governments should negotiate to lock in market access during the good times so as to safeguard against trade restrictions when the economy turns sour. Canadian federal and provincial governments had to work extremely hard just to get a narrow and last-minute deal to exempt Canadian companies from "Buy American" provisions in the

U.S. stimulus package. By then, much of the stimulus cash had already been allocated. That experience provides a good reminder of the difficulties of counteracting such actions after they have already been launched. Canada should lock in reductions to trade barriers now, in order to avoid such situations in future.

> **Governments should negotiate to lock in market access during the good times in order to safeguard against trade restrictions when the economy turns sour.**

AN INTEGRATIVE TRADE POLICY

Unlike in the past, today's public policies should not focus solely on opening up markets for final goods exports. The rise of global supply chains, the ability to sell services increasingly around the world, the ability to trade and collaborate electronically, the greater global movement of people and ideas, and the acceleration of foreign affiliate sales call for policies that allow businesses to seize this broader range of opportunities.

> **Canadian policy-makers face the challenge of maintaining and enhancing access to the U.S. market in the face of protectionism.**

An integrative trade policy requires a change in mindset. It means removing barriers—not just to trade, but to investment; not just for goods, but for services; and not just for exports, but for imported inputs and technologies. Free-trade agreements should go beyond eliminating traditional goods tariffs to recognize the barriers facing this broader range of activities. Current Canada–European Union free trade negotiations, for example, cover such areas as services trade and labour mobility.

An integrative trade policy also means taking actions at home that are critical to global success—such as eliminating interprovincial trade and labour mobility barriers, investing in infrastructure, and putting measures in place to address the short-term adjustments that some sectors and individuals will face.

Deep global linkages may also increase public support for adopting integrative trade policies, thereby giving leaders the policy room needed not only to resist protectionist actions, but also to proactively remove a wide range of existing trade and investment barriers.

CONCLUSION

While the collapse of international trade and global supply chains likely pulled us more deeply into recession than would otherwise have been the case, expanded integrative trade can help position us for future growth. Tight global linkages may help counteract protectionist brakes on that trade expansion. But for companies and countries to realize the full benefits of trade, policy-makers first need to do no harm. This means resisting further protectionist impulses. Next, they must go on the offensive by adopting integrative trade policies that are in line with the realities of today's globally integrated production.

For the best global economic results, leaders need to learn the lessons of the past and collectively resist putting up new trade barriers. They need to continue working together to eliminate existing barriers, with the goal of eventually putting one set of global trade rules in place. Unfortunately, global trade talks are limping along, and some leaders and countries have succumbed to protectionist measures. Smart policy-makers will not wait for collective action. Countries that build on the mitigating effect of global integration and open themselves further to integrative trade will give their companies a head start as the economy recovers. These countries will also be doing their part for the collective good. Those who seek a return to protectionism are only shooting themselves, their economies, and the world economy in the foot.

LESSON 8

Local Governments Can Best Respond to a Recession by Staying the Course

by *Mario Lefebvre*

HIGHLIGHTS

- The ability to provide support during tougher economic times depends on having the means to help—and local governments simply do not have the stimulus tools to help during a recession.

- The "no deficit" rule makes it difficult for Canada's local governments to offer any kind of relief through additional spending.

- Infrastructure investment must be the number one priority for cities over the coming years.

- The best strategy for local governments is to work hard to make their cities attractive to immigrants and investment—and when recessions strike, to stay the course.

While the recession showed that government stimulus can effectively provide support in lifting the economy out of its doldrums, not all levels of government are equal when it comes to such help. The simple fact is that the ability to provide support during tougher economic times depends on having the means to help— and local governments do not have the stimulus tools to help during a recession. Although they are well able to provide current services and to design and implement long-term infrastructure requirements, local governments are not well-suited to addressing short-term economic fluctuations. Aggregate counter-cyclical policy, therefore, must take place at higher levels of government.

To play a significant role during hard economic times, a government must possess the necessary fiscal tools. What concrete fiscal tools do local governments have? Two come immediately to mind: property taxes and user fees. Only the former generates significant revenues for local governments, so let's see how property taxes could be used to stimulate the economy.

The "no deficit" rule makes it difficult for Canada's local governments to offer any kind of relief through additional spending.

Consider a hypothetical case in which a local government decides to offer a 5 per cent rebate on property taxes to help its citizens weather the financial storm. While that sounds generous, it would produce a saving of only $100 on an average residential property tax bill of $2,000. Moreover, homeowners usually pay their property tax bill in at least two payments. So households would get a tax break of $50 in, say, January and another $50 in July—not a lot of additional purchasing power, and not all of it would be spent on goods and services. The same logic applies to user fees. Lowering the costs of attending a city-run class, or cutting the hourly rental rate at a hockey rink, would leave only a few extra dollars in people's pockets.

Although this type of tax relief would provide little stimulus to the economy, it would dig a substantial revenue hole for local governments, as property taxes remain their chief source of revenue. Plus, there is a catch—local governments are generally forbidden from running deficits. Therefore, a proposed property tax break would have to be offset by an equivalent cut in operating expenditures, which could offset the tax break's positive economic impact on the economy. For example, local governments would have to leave snow on the ground longer or pick up garbage only every second week—meaning less money for snow-removal or waste-collection companies. In any case, citizens would be unlikely to appreciate such actions, making a property tax break unappealing politically.

While it could be argued that a 5 per cent property tax break would not bring a whole lot of relief to households, firms would applaud a significant reduction in the property taxes they pay. But again, if City Hall offers a tax break to struggling firms during a recession, how will it make up for the loss in revenues in order to balance its budget?

The "no deficit" rule also makes it difficult for Canada's local governments to offer any kind of relief through additional spending. For example, most cities now handle economic development duties. An appropriate counter-cyclical response during a recession would be to increase these expenditures to promote economic development. But if a city were to decide to do so, it would have to offset this additional spending by reducing expenditures in other areas—thus restoring the legally mandated balanced budget and, potentially, offsetting the economic benefits of the extra spending in economic development. An alternative to slashing spending elsewhere would be to increase property taxes to boost revenues in line with the increased spending on development. However, that path makes no sense during a recession.

It is often argued that Canadian cities should be offered a different set of revenue-generating tools—for example, the right to collect income or consumption-based taxes. While The Conference Board of Canada agrees that Canadian cities do need a diverse set of revenue-generating tools, it must be emphasized that income and consumption-based taxes are much more cyclical than property taxes and are therefore of little help in the kind of tough economic times we saw in 2008–09.

In the United States, where local governments do have access to such cyclical revenue-generating tools, municipalities did indeed witness a decline in revenues just when they needed them most to stimulate the local economy. For example, local governments' revenues in the U.S. declined by 2.8 per cent in the second quarter of 2009 from a year earlier, mostly due to a decline in local income tax and sales tax collections.[1] Such a decline in revenues, if applied in the Canadian context where

---

1   Dadayan and Boyd, *State Revenue Report*, 1.

local governments are not allowed to run deficits, would force local governments to either cut spending or increase other taxes in order to balance their budgets.

Our advice for citizens and firms during difficult economic times is: Do not look to City Hall for help—its hands are tied. And our advice for city halls during difficult economic times is: Do not lose sight of your long-term objectives—you simply do not have the fiscal tools required to deal with short-term economic disruptions. City halls, instead, should focus on such things as putting together infrastructure investment plans and economic development strategies, and finding ways to attract immigrants to their communities. In the current post-recession context, infrastructure investment should be a short-term objective, and economic development strategies and attracting immigrants can be medium-to-long-term targets.

Infrastructure investment must be the number one priority for cities over the coming years. There are plenty of federal and provincial programs now available, and local governments must be involved. Infrastructure is a great way for cities to invest under some of the current programs—every dollar they spend on infrastructure can turn into as much as three dollars of investment. That's because several federal and provincial programs are designed in such a way that if a city invests one dollar, the federal and provincial governments each invest a dollar of their own.

Investment spending at the city level is not included in the operating deficit, and therefore will not break the "no deficit" rule. Of course, increased interest payments as a result of the additional infrastructure spending and related debt will add to the city's operating deficit in subsequent years—again suggesting that there is a limit to the amount of money local governments can invest. But when an outlay of one dollar leads to a three-dollar investment (as it does under some current programs), and when interest rates are as low as they have been, the time is as right as it will ever be to take on added debt burden.

Economic development is also a crucial part of our local governments' mandate. In fact, Canada's cities have played an increasing role with respect to economic development over the years. But their role is not one of short-term support—it is not about providing an immediate lift to, for example, an industry that is struggling because of an economic downturn. The role of local governments is to provide *long-term* planning. It is about aligning the city's long-term planning process with the structure of the economy. In other words, once a city has identified the industries that drive the area's economic activity, the city must incorporate into its planning process measures that will suit the long-term needs of those industries. These include, for example, the expansion of industrial parks, ensuring that the proper infrastructure is in place, and building the right types of homes to ensure that the local industries are able to attract and retain the workers they need.

> **The bottom line is that attracting immigrants will be key to the future of our cities, and our country as a whole.**

Attracting people must be another one of our cities' prime long-term objectives. The population is aging and population growth is slowing. Any city that is not successful at attracting people can look forward to a very bleak future. The ability to attract people is not driven solely by a strong economy. Access to health care and educational facilities, a low crime rate, and a wide range of cultural activities are but a few of the non-economic factors that make a city attractive.

Globally, almost every developed country today faces the challenge of an aging population, and that means the battle for immigrants has already begun. Cities, of course, are not alone into this battle. The federal and provincial governments will also have to step in with strategies to attract immigrants. So will professional associations, since recognizing credentials is one of the issues at play in attracting immigrants. The bottom line is that attracting immigrants will be key to the future of our cities, and our country as a whole.

At the city level, attracting people is not confined to pulling in new immigrants who are searching for the best place in which to begin their new lives in Canada. Drawing people from other cities within the same province or from other provinces is also good for the receiving city (though not so good for the donor city).

Overall, the best strategy for our local governments is to work hard to make their cities appealing to immigrants, new residents, and investment—and when recessions strike, to stay the course. While it may be tempting in times of economic turmoil to jump in to help, ultimately, a steady path remains a local government's best option.

CONCLUSION

Local officials would love to help in times of recession. Who can blame them? These are the elected men and women closest to the population, who see and hear first-hand the impact of a recession on their neighbours and citizens. It is human nature to want to give a hand when you see that your neighbour is struggling.

Unfortunately, local officials do not have the fiscal tools to help. The "no deficit" clause that hangs over their heads keeps them from taking significant stimulus action. Indeed, The Conference Board of Canada advises local officials to avoid the temptation to try to help by providing exceptional stimulus spending. Their best action in times of turmoil is simply to stay the course. They should keep working on the long-term foundations of their community, such as sound infrastructure, and on making their cities attractive to newcomers and investors. This is the best way to ensure that future recessions—and there will be other recessions—affect their community as little as possible.

LESSON 9
Psychology Helps Dictate How Recessions Unfold

by *Christopher Beckman*

HIGHLIGHTS

- One possible reason why most forecasters failed to anticipate the downturn is that conventional economic thinking has a fundamental flaw—the belief that people think and act rationally.

- The conviction among many Americans that housing prices would always increase convinced others to go along with this fallacy—and before long, millions of people believed something that would indeed soon prove to be entirely false.

- It is this psychological dimension of recession that makes an early and strong intervention by monetary and fiscal authorities all the more important.

A key—but often overlooked—factor in assessing the causes of the recession is the important role that psychology plays in determining how economic events unfold. Some economists contend that one reason why most forecasters failed to anticipate the downturn is that conventional economic thinking has a fundamental flaw—the belief that people think and act rationally. That failure to account for simple human nature and psychology led even some of the greatest minds in economics to overlook the coming storm. In 2004, the Chairman of the Federal Reserve at the time, Alan Greenspan, declared that a housing bubble was unlikely since markets operated very efficiently. About the same time, current Chairman Ben Bernanke was saying that soaring home prices were simply a reflection of the strong underlying fundamentals.

The great British economist John Maynard Keynes (1883–1946) touched on the impact that psychology has on the economy when he used the term "animal spirits" to help explain the ups and downs in business and consumer confidence. Keynes contended that swings in confidence were not always logical, and that business cycles were often driven by emotional responses—animal spirits.[1] During good economic times, he argued, people have significant trust and confidence in economic developments and a sense of euphoria that leads them to make decisions spontaneously. In good times, people believe that they will succeed regardless of the underlying risks, and they often ignore warning signs that trouble is around the bend.

> **The psychology of recession becomes a self-fulfilling prophecy—if people feel bad about their economic prospects, then things do indeed get worse.**

Conversely, in bad economic times, consumers and investors can be easily discouraged by all the talk of recession and gloom and doom. Their attitude turns negative, and they suffer a drop in confidence— a change that leads consumers and businesses to buy and invest less. People hunker down. As they slash personal and investment spending in an effort to husband their cash, they weaken the economy even further through a pullback in aggregate demand. The psychology of recession becomes a self-fulfilling prophecy—if people feel bad about their economic prospects, then things do indeed get worse.

The effect that psychology can have on markets was clearly on display during the unsustainable run-up in housing markets in the middle part of this past decade. Yale's Robert Shiller was one of the few economists to anticipate the U.S. housing bust years before it happened. He contends that the surge in home prices marked a period in which confidence in

---

1   Keynes, *The General Theory of Employment, Interest, and Money*, 161–162.

the economy was not based on rational behaviour.[2] The faith in U.S. mortgage and housing markets caused home prices to soar to unsustainable levels—a vivid example of Keynes' "animal spirits" racing out of control. Psychologists use the term "herding" to describe the fact that if a large number of people believe something, then others are convinced it must be true. Everyone thought home prices could only go up even though, historically, this has never been the case. The belief among many Americans that housing prices always increase convinced others to go along with this fallacy—and before long, millions of people believed something that would indeed soon prove to be entirely false. Given this line of thinking, the ensuing housing bubble and collapse was almost inevitable.

The hyperbolic tone of news coverage and stock market volatility almost certainly contributed to the increasing pessimism among Canadians.

Complex financial instruments, such as collateralized debt obligations and credit default swaps, made the situation even worse. When people have trouble understanding something, as they did with these instruments, they frequently forgo their own judgment and follow the lead of others. If home prices can only go higher, why not take out an even bigger mortgage and use the home equity to buy a large flat-screen TV or to go on an expensive vacation? This kind of thinking also led banks to sell easy-term mortgages to people who had no chance of repaying the loan if home prices stopped accelerating. Not surprisingly, the consequences were disastrous.

In Canada, the impacts that psychology can have on the economy were readily apparent in the fall of 2008. The Canadian economy continued to create jobs right though to October, and the economy actually expanded in the third quarter of 2008, albeit at a very weak pace. The recession was still in the future. Yet in October 2008, The Conference

---

2   Shiller, "Animal Spirits Depend on Trust."

Board of Canada's consumer confidence index fell to its lowest point since the third quarter of 1982—a time when the Canadian economy was mired in recession. The hyperbolic tone of news coverage and stock market volatility almost certainly contributed to the increasing pessimism among Canadians, which in turn had a negative effect on consumer spending. Even though economic conditions in Canada were not that bad—and certainly not as bad as in the U.S.—growth in real spending in Canada in the fall of 2008 flattened out and then declined.

Appropriate regulation would have ensured that investors purchased properly assessed derivatives where the risk was clearly spelled out.

An important lesson from the recession is that since people do not always make rational decisions, especially when it comes to the economy, intervention by government is justified to ensure that human psychology doesn't derail the economy completely. Strong government regulation of financial markets is essential to ensure that we don't experience the type of panic that erupted in the fall of 2008. Panic and fear set in among investors when the value of their investments, which many didn't fully understand, started to drop. These frightened investors rushed to unload all of their mortgage-backed securities, as well as other assets—even those that were not in danger. Appropriate regulation would have ensured that investors purchased properly assessed derivatives where the risk was clearly spelled out. As Shiller notes, a brilliant hockey player requires a referee to ensure that the rules are followed in a way that enables the player to reveal his or her true talents. Similarly, the capitalist system needs a referee—in this case, the government—to ensure that the free-market economy operates in as efficient a manner as possible, and that the psychology of fear remains dormant.

It is this psychological dimension of recessions that makes an early and strong intervention by monetary and fiscal authorities all the more important. Policy intervention can help dampen the effects of a recession. There is little doubt that the dramatic steps taken by governments and monetary authorities all over the world in the fall of 2008 saved us from a far worse fate—a prolonged recession, or possibly even another Great Depression. Governments are seldom perfect, and mistakes were made. (Probably the most damaging error was allowing global financial giant Lehman Brothers to fail in September 2008.) In general, however, the policy steps that were implemented did help to restore confidence. Consumer confidence in Canada, for instance, began to rebound strongly in February 2009; and, while sentiment faltered in the spring of 2010 (due in part to the credit crisis in Europe), it has remained far above the lows seen in the fall of 2008.

The important role that human psychology can play in the economy is often overlooked by economists when they assess the causes of severe recessions such as the one we have just lived through. Given the events of 2008 and 2009, this kind of oversight should not be allowed to happen again. And if we ever need a reminder of the influence of psychology on the economy, we can think back to Franklin Roosevelt and the famous line from his 1933 inaugural U.S. presidential address: "The only thing we have to fear is fear itself." Those were prophetic words at the time, and they still ring true in the 21st century.

LESSON 10
The Fiscal Bills Will Have to Be Paid

by *Matthew Stewart*

HIGHLIGHTS

- Despite the global economic recovery, many countries are saddled with heavy debt loads that will constrain their ability to fund programs for years to come. These countries now face a loss of investor confidence if they do not begin to implement credible plans to reduce their fiscal deficits.
- Overall government debt in the EU is expected to skyrocket—from an average of 58.8 per cent of GDP before the crisis to an estimated 83.8 per cent in 2011. This will make it even more difficult for EU governments to meet the increasing and costly demands of an aging population.
- Canada has emerged from the recession in a much better fiscal position than almost every other developed country. Years of paying down debt prior to the recession are now paying dividends for the federal government.
- For many provincial governments, their ability to balance their books is contingent on controlling health-care costs.

In 2008, the world was plunged into its worst financial crisis since the 1930s. In a concerted effort to limit the damage caused by the financial collapse, governments around the globe endorsed and introduced massive fiscal stimulus, combined with exceptional monetary stimulus. Many countries—even those that were already running sizable deficits before the crisis struck—ramped up spending and cut taxes. As tax revenues plunged and stimulus packages averaging 2 per cent of GDP in 2009 and 1.5 per cent in 2010 kicked in, deficits ballooned. In 2009, net borrowing in advanced countries reached an unsustainable 8.7 per cent of GDP.[1] In Europe, deficits soared past the EU's mandated 3 per cent limit to reach 6.8 per cent of GDP. Although countries such as the United Kingdom and Germany are now enacting program restraint and tax increases, deficit ratios among the EU countries are expected to improve only marginally over the next few years.

For countries that fail to rein in their debt, the consequences will be serious.

As growth returns, many countries are still saddled with heavy debt loads that will constrain their ability to fund programs for years to come. These countries now face a loss of investor confidence if they do not begin to implement credible plans to reduce their fiscal deficits. At the same time, there is great risk that any premature withdrawal of stimulus could endanger the economic recovery and push their economies back into recession. Countries that have ignored rising debt levels for years (Greece being perhaps the starkest example) face particularly difficult decisions. Many will be forced to reform their economies and labour markets to encourage economic growth while at the same time introducing substantial tax increases and slashing social and other programs. For countries that fail to rein in their debt, the consequences will be serious— credit downgrades, rising interest costs, currency devaluation, and the risk of financial shocks. These consequences of high debt are already being felt in several European countries, particularly in Portugal, Ireland, Italy, Greece, and Spain. Governments there have been forced to implement urgent reforms—reforms that many find hard to swallow.

Another challenge lies ahead for developed nations. Aging populations are slowing government revenue growth while simultaneously increasing the demand for health care, government pensions, and other spending. The United Nations estimates that in the more developed regions,[2] the share of the population over the age of 65 is expected to

---

1   International Monetary Fund, "World Economic Outlook Database."

2   The United Nations defines "more developed regions" as all regions of Europe, plus North America, Australia, New Zealand, and Japan.

rise on average from 15.9 per cent of the population today to 26.2 per cent by 2030. The demographic outlook is particularly dire in Greece, Italy, Spain, and Japan—all countries with high and rising debt levels.

The lesson for governments as the recovery becomes more firmly entrenched is that they simply cannot afford to continue to run fiscal deficits and drive up debt as before. The time has come to make some tough choices on rebalancing the books.

THE EUROPEAN SITUATION

In the EU, rising debt levels have become a cause of great concern to investors, governments, and the public alike. Before the 2008–09 financial crisis, many EU governments were running sizable deficits and had been doing so for years, building up significant debt burdens. Although average new net annual borrowing in the EU had declined to 0.8 per cent of GDP in 2007, in the five preceding years it had averaged 2.5 per cent of GDP a year.[3] This continuous borrowing had pushed average debt levels in the EU to 58.8 per cent of GDP—very close to the EU's mandated limit of 60 per cent. Moreover, within the eurozone itself, average debt levels had already shot past the 60 per cent threshold to reach 66 per cent by 2007. That left governments with little room to manoeuvre in the financial crises that followed.

When the global financial crisis struck in late 2008, revenues quickly began to fall and automatic stabilizers, such as unemployment benefits, rapidly increased. On top of that, as the global economy fell into recession, many countries decided their best course would be to try to spend their way out of the crisis. As a consequence, government deficits in the EU reached an average of 6.8 per cent of GDP in 2009, and that figure is expected to rise to 7.2 per cent in 2010.[4] Furthermore, the European Commission estimates that the structural deficit (the deficit that would exist if the economy were operating at full potential) for EU members

---

3   European Commission, *European Economic Forecast—Spring 2010*, 200.

4   Ibid.

will reach 5.6 per cent of GDP in 2010, suggesting that even once their economies have fully recovered, deep spending cuts, large tax hikes, or a combination of the two will still be needed to bring deficits back down to sustainable levels.

Given the rapid increase in deficits, it's not surprising that overall government debt in the EU is expected to skyrocket—from an average of 58.8 per cent of GDP before the crisis to an estimated 83.8 per cent in 2011, a staggering 25 percentage point increase. This will make it even more difficult for EU governments to meet the increasing and costly demands of an aging population.

In Greece and Italy, debt-to-GDP ratios have surpassed the 100 per cent mark, and several more countries are heading in that direction.

Adding to Europe's troubles is the fact that debt levels in several member countries have already reached unsustainable levels. In Greece and Italy, debt-to-GDP ratios have surpassed the 100 per cent mark, and several more countries are heading in that direction. Bond rating agencies have responded by downgrading several countries' debt, which in turn has raised investors' fears and pushed up the risk premium that must be paid in the form of higher interest rates. The situation is particularly grave in Greece, whose debt has been downgraded to junk status over fears that the government will default. The Greek crisis forced the EU and the International Monetary Fund to provide Greece with €110 billion in emergency funding. As well, the EU created a €500-billion stabilization fund aimed at preventing the crisis from spreading to Portugal, Spain, and Ireland. The IMF contributed a further €250 billion to the fund. Greece has been forced to accept stringent conditions. In return for the EU and IMF help, the government has had to cut spending, reduce bonuses, increase the retirement age, and raise taxes—moves that have been deeply unpopular with many Greeks. Even with these measures in place, fiscal deficits will continue until 2014, and the debt will continue to rise. Moreover, fears remain that Greece will need additional funds or debt restructuring.

Although the emergency funding has so far succeeded in preventing the crisis from spreading, additional tough action will be required if the EU is to address the root of the problem and prevent member countries from plunging back into crisis. With the worst offenders now able to borrow from the EU and the IMF at below-market rates, there may be even less incentive to make the required changes and ensure fiscal discipline. In response to this threat, the EU is attempting to crack down on countries that don't abide by EU deficit targets. The European Commission (the EU's executive arm) has recommended that it now scrutinize members' spending plans before those plans get passed by their national parliaments, and that the commission be given increased powers to punish countries that break the rules. This would be a monumental change to the EU structure, but it may be the only way to prevent some countries from continuing to live beyond their means.

THE U.K. AND THE U.S.

Britain's fiscal situation is grave. Although the country's debt-to-GDP ratio was a relatively low 44 per cent of GDP before the crisis, the government was already dealing with a large structural fiscal deficit. Program spending in Britain (which is not part of the eurozone) had been close to running out of control. In the 10 years before the recession, among comparable countries, Britain posted the fastest increase in public spending as a share of national income.[5] During the recession—with revenues collapsing, automatic stabilizers ramping up, and the government enacting a sizable stimulus plan—the deficit soared, reaching a stunning 13 per cent of GDP in fiscal 2009–10.[6] According to the IMF, without significant action, Britain's debt-to-GDP levels would have almost doubled

---

5   Crawford, Emmerson, and Tetlow, *A Survey of Public Spending in the U.K.*, 6.

6   European Commission, *Public Finance in the EMU.*

by 2014—to 87.8 per cent. Moreover, there has been concern that Britain's credit rating could fall, which would result in higher borrowing and debt-servicing costs, thus making it even more difficult for the government to balance its books.

When the new British coalition government took office in May, it immediately came under pressure to take action to contain the deficit. Although the government has vowed to protect health spending, the health sector alone accounts for nearly a third of all departmental budgets. As such, a combination of tax hikes and determined restraint in all non-health spending categories is needed. Over the next five years, the government plans to make cuts in public spending equal to about 4.7 per cent of GDP, and it will raise taxes by the equivalent of almost 1.6 per cent of GDP. While the most notable tax hike is the increase in the value-added tax (VAT), which will rise to 20 per cent from 17.5 per cent, other increases are planned as well. On the spending side, outside of protected areas, spending will have to fall by an astounding 25 per cent to achieve the target of a balanced budget by 2014–15. There is no doubt that following through on these cuts will be extremely difficult; but Britain can take pride in being one of the few countries so far to accept the necessity of such tough actions.

In the United States, government deficits have also risen to unsustainable levels. By 2008, the cost of fighting two wars while cutting taxes on upper-income earners was taking a toll. That year, the federal deficit rose to 6.6 per cent of GDP.[7] In 2009, with the recession eating away at tax revenues and the government trying to spend the economy back to health, the fiscal deficit soared to 12.5 per cent of GDP. The result is that the federal government's net debt will rise to 66.2 per cent of GDP this year—and it is currently on course to climb to 85.5 per cent by 2015 if no action is taken. Although that level of debt to GDP is still lower than what we see today in many countries in Europe, it represents a huge jump. The ratio has already increased by more than half from 2006 when it stood at 41.9 per cent.

---

7 International Monetary Fund, *World Economic Outlook*, 169.

As the temporary stimulus plan is removed from U.S. federal spending beginning in 2010–11, the deficit will begin to decline. Recent IMF projections have placed the deficit at 6.5 per cent of GDP in 2015, absent further action. However, the Obama administration says it intends to narrow the deficit further through a three-year freeze on non-security discretionary spending.

Clearly, bold action will be required, but the political conditions for such boldness do not yet exist.

At first glance, the U.S. fiscal situation appears to be improving. However, like many other Western countries, the U.S. will also have to deal with the effects of an aging population. As the baby boomers begin to retire, upward pressure on federal spending for such programs as Medicare and Medicaid will steadily increase. According to Medicare's board of trustees, to cover all of Medicare's unfunded liabilities, the federal government would have to raise payroll taxes today by the equivalent of 6.8 per cent of GDP.[8] A similar situation exists for Social Security, where the board of trustees estimates that the payroll tax would have to rise by the equivalent of 1.3 per cent of GDP immediately to cover the program's unfunded liability.[9] The Congressional Budget Office estimates that the government deficit will narrow over the next decade, but because of the aging population and rising health costs will begin to rise again to reach 15 per cent of GDP by 2035. Under this status quo scenario, net debt would exceed an unsustainable 180 per cent of GDP in 2035.[10] Clearly, bold action will be required, but the political conditions for such boldness do not yet exist.

---

8   Boards of Trustees of the Federal Hospital Insurance and Federal Supplementary Medical Insurance Trust Funds, *The 2009 Annual Report* (Washington, DC: Boards of Trustees of the Federal Hospital Insurance and Federal Supplementary Medical Insurance Trust Funds, 2009).

9   Board of Trustees of the Federal Old-Age and Survivors Insurance and Federal Disability Insurance Trust Funds, *The 2009 Annual Report* (Washington, DC: Board of Trustees of the Federal Old-Age and Survivors Insurance and Federal Disability Insurance Trust Funds, 2009).

10 Congressional Budget Office, *The Long-Term Budget Outlook—June 2010.*

WHY IS JAPAN SO DIFFERENT?

Japan has the highest debt-to-GDP ratio of any advanced country. In Europe, countries are encouraged to maintain debt-to-GDP levels of 60 per cent or less. Yet, since the financial crisis hit, Japan has seen its public debt increase to over 200 per cent of GDP. Despite having such a frightening level of debt, the Japanese government enjoys the lowest interest rate in the world. A two-year government bond, for example, yields just 0.15 per cent. How is that possible, when countries such as Greece find themselves forced to offer yields 30 or 40 times higher? The difference is that almost all of Japan's government debt is held by its own citizens. Consequently, there is little risk of outright default, since the Japanese government could, as a last resort, simply print money to pay its obligations to its citizens. However, one lesson we can take from Europe's recent debt crisis is that even in Japan, debt levels cannot increase forever. Unless Japan begins to get its financial house in order, severe difficulties await.

Japan's population is already older than that of any other country, and it continues to age faster than the populations in most other developed countries. By 2050, almost 38 per cent of Japan's citizens will be over the age of 65, up from an already high 23 per cent today.[11] As more Japanese retire, there will be fewer savings available for buying government bonds—and without large increases in domestic savings, the government will not be able to sell the vast amount of government bonds it needs to fund its deficit. Moreover, if bondholders see increased risk of inflation, they too will demand higher returns or seek out better yields in the international market. And if the Japanese government has to sell more of its bonds on the world market, it will find itself in an increasingly difficult situation. Already, 35 per cent of government revenues go toward paying interest costs on the debt. If rates were to rise even modestly, interest payments would soar, potentially resulting in a crisis.

---

11 Population Division of the Department of Economic and Social Affairs of the United Nations Secretariat, *World Population Prospects*.

CANADIAN FISCAL OUTLOOK

Canada entered the recession on a much better fiscal footing than most other developed countries, thanks to a decade-long string of surpluses and falling debt ratios. However, the need for fiscal stimulus coupled with a precipitous drop in revenues meant that Canada was not immune to deficits and rising debt. The ratio of all federal and provincial debt to GDP has risen substantially—from 50 per cent in 2008–09 to an estimated 60 per cent in 2010–11.

The federal and provincial stories will begin to diverge in the coming years. At the federal level, debt paid down over the decade leading up to the recession has given the federal government room to manoeuvre over the medium term. By around 2015, with the economy fully recovered from the recession, we expect the federal books to be back in balance. Many provincial governments, however, will struggle to balance their books over that period. These provinces face slowing revenue growth— and because health care is a provincial responsibility, all will have to cope with the rising health-care costs associated with an aging population. Ontario—which was hit particularly hard by the recession—has the biggest hill to climb in eliminating its deficits.

The three main sources of federal revenues—personal income tax, corporate income tax, and indirect taxes (largely the goods and services tax)—all suffered steep declines in 2009. Coupled with the federal stimulus plan, the result was a large deficit and a big run-up in federal debt. In his October 2010 update of the federal government's budget projections, Finance Minister Jim Flaherty said the 2009–10 deficit had come in at a record $55.6 billion—almost $2 billion higher than forecast in his March budget. However, he also said the deficit for 2010–11 would be $45.5 billion, or $3.7 billion lower than forecast in the budget. Based on the government's promise of aggressive spending restraint and on its forecast of rising revenues, the deficit is projected to steadily decline, shrinking to $1.7 billion by 2014–15.

In fact, the future now looks even brighter than what the finance minister is projecting. The Conference Board of Canada expects nominal GDP growth in 2010 to exceed the consensus view used in the federal budget. That expectation has been supported by recent estimates from Statistics Canada. Nominal GDP is now expected to expand by 6.3 per cent in 2010, considerably stronger than the budget's consensus forecast of 4.9 per cent. If spending restraint can be kept on track, the federal government should be able to balance its books up to a year earlier than projected.

Still, the series of expected federal deficits will add almost $160 billion to the stock of federal debt by 2014—erasing a decade of debt payback. Even so, Canada will reap benefits from the 11 years of fiscal surpluses achieved before the recession, when the federal debt ratio declined from 68.4 per cent of GDP in 1995–96 to just 29 per cent in 2008–09. This performance left Canada with a much stronger fiscal foundation than that of nearly every other major industrial country. Moreover, recent positive developments—notably, the smaller-than-projected deficit for 2009–10 and stronger nominal income growth in 2010—mean that the federal debt ratio will peak at about 35 per cent in 2010–11, still well within manageable levels.

Provincial governments, on the other hand, face bigger challenges. Their corporate and personal income tax revenues also shrank during the recession, and the incentive to match federal infrastructure spending to help kick-start their economies was somewhat of a mixed blessing. Newfoundland, Saskatchewan, Alberta, and British Columbia faced an additional challenge—sharply lower commodity prices reduced their revenues from royalties. In 2008, combined royalty revenues stood at $23.1 billion. Only one year later, they had fallen to $10.2 billion. As a whole, provincial governments have estimated their collective deficit at almost $34 billion in the 2009–10 fiscal year. That number is not expected to improve much any time soon. The estimate for 2010–11 is $32 billion.

In contrast to the federal government, the deficits run by some provinces are more structural in nature. During the good economic times before 2008, many provinces ramped up expenditures on things like health care, rather than pay off debt. Consequently, the sharp loss in revenues during the recession, combined with rising health-care costs, implies that the provinces face very difficult decisions over the medium term in their battle to regain fiscal health. Their choice is simple: increase taxes or severely restrain growth in expenditures. Holding back spending will be extremely challenging and could require structural changes in how services are delivered, given the health-care demands of an aging population and the political weight of the largest cohort—the baby boomers.

Provincial governments have increased health-care spending over the last five years by an average of 7 per cent a year (in current dollars). An aging population means more and more people will be retiring, which in turn means provincial revenue growth will slow substantially, putting even more pressure on the provinces to control costs. For many provincial governments, achieving balanced budgets depends crucially on their ability to control health-care costs. This is particularly true in Ontario, where plans to shrink the deficit are contingent on limiting health-care spending growth to just 3 per cent a year. With health-care demand pressures set to rapidly increase, slowing the recent pace of health-care spending growth will be a major challenge.

CONCLUSION

The severity of the financial crisis, the collapse in confidence, and the resulting recession called for dramatic measures on a global scale. Governments around the world responded with incredible levels of monetary and fiscal stimulus. Now the time has come to start paying the bills. As the recovery becomes more firmly entrenched, governments will have to face up to fiscal reality and begin implementing the tough but necessary measures needed to get their deficits and debt under control.

For some countries, the financial crisis has pushed already-high debt obligations to unsustainable levels, and investors have lost confidence in the capacity of these countries to service their public debt. This is true for Greece and others in southern Europe, where immediate action must be taken to rebuild confidence. To do that, they must reduce their fiscal deficits and begin to dismantle structural barriers in their labour markets. These actions would help to create better conditions for sustainable economic growth. If these countries fail to get their fiscal houses in order, credit down-grades will be inevitable—resulting in higher interest rates and the risk of financial shocks, which would weaken or even cripple any recovery.

Canada has emerged from the recession in a much stronger fiscal position than almost every other developed country. Years of paying down debt before the recession are now paying dividends for the federal government. Despite all the stimulus spending, the federal debt-to-GDP ratio will peak at a relatively low 35 per cent in 2010–11. Strong growth in nominal income this year, combined with the federal government's planned spending restraint, has put the government on track to balance its books by 2014–15—a full year ahead of schedule.

Canada's provinces face a more difficult challenge. Like the federal government, they ran up large deficits during the recession. The difference is that spending restraint will be much harder for provincial governments. In 2009–10, health care consumed over 40 cents of every dollar spent (excluding debt payments). Health-care spending has averaged an unsustainable 7.1 per cent annual growth over the last five years, and 7.5 per cent over the five years before that. With an aging population putting pressure on both revenues and expenditures, the only long-term fiscally sustainable solution is to boost productivity growth in the health-care system. This is indeed a difficult challenge, but the alternatives are higher taxes, increased wait times, or rationing of health care.

CONCLUSION
Extraordinary Times . . . Extraordinary Measures

by *Glen Hodgson*

Extraordinary times demand extraordinary measures. In the fall of 2008, governments around the world responded to a once-in-a-lifetime global financial crisis and to the resulting recession by taking exceptional action on numerous fronts. They needed to act swiftly and almost simultaneously.

If there was a major error in the intervention strategy, it came in the very early days of the crisis with the failure of investment banking giant Lehman Brothers. Rather than intervening to keep Lehman Brothers intact—as Washington had already done with Bear Stearns in the spring of 2008 and Merrill Lynch earlier in September 2008 when they were in deep financial trouble—the U.S. government allowed Lehman Brothers to fail. The bankruptcy unleashed waves of fear and financial loss that rippled through the entire global financial system.

The fear factor unleashed by the failure of Lehman Brothers created a severe systemic shock. Governments managed to contain the systemic risk in the financial sector by building a floor under the global financial system. They did this through coordinated national intervention in the form of nationalization in whole or in part, equity injections, and guarantees as required. Similar intervention was eventually undertaken in the U.S. auto sector, bringing order to a chaotic situation in that market segment. Central banks used monetary policy aggressively to provide exceptional levels of liquidity and stave off deflation. Governments injected massive amounts of fiscal stimulus to help restore confidence and to kick-start economic growth.

For the most part, the plan worked. Specific measures were implemented in a coordinated, orderly, and pragmatic way. When something didn't work (like the efforts to strip bad mortgage assets out of U.S. banks), the strategy was quickly adjusted to find some other form of intervention that would. Thanks to the massive concerted action, confidence in the global financial system has been rebuilt—steadily but unevenly—and the global economy has sputtered back to life. The global economic and financial system remains fraught with risk and uncertainty, as demonstrated by the shock to investor confidence caused by the Greek financial tragedy in the spring of 2010. But growth has returned, and step-by-step healing is under way.

Members of The Conference Board of Canada's Forecasting and Analysis team extracted ten key lessons from the financial crisis and recession.

- Fiscal stimulus can take credit for helping Canada return to economic growth. Working with a highly accommodative monetary policy, fiscal stimulus helped mitigate the worst of the recession and kick-start the economy.
- The recession and accompanying increase in unemployment provided only temporary reprieve from Canada's tight labour market conditions. Looming skill shortages have implications for labour market policies in all forms.
- The financial sector is not just a sector like the others, since it provides a critical service to all parts of the economy. The financial sector, therefore, must be treated differently, with a strong and clear regulatory structure and with a higher degree of transparency in its operations and the risks it takes.
- Strong and engaged public sector financial institutions can help significantly to fill gaps in the private financial system when a crisis does hit.
- In times of economic crisis, global policy coordination is critical to a recovery, given the deeply interconnected nature of the global economy today.

- Firms can be "too big to fail"—with catastrophic costs to an economy. As a consequence, it is in the public interest to act before any crisis to limit the systemic risk posed by very large firms.
- International trade helped pull Canada and the world into recession, but deep global linkages may have blunted the protectionist response. These links can help the Canadian and global economies better position themselves coming out of the recession.
- Local governments may have the will to help pull an economy out of recession—unfortunately, they do not have the fiscal tools.
- Consumer and investor psychology plays an important role in determining how economic events unfold.
- As the recovery becomes more firmly entrenched, governments must face the new fiscal reality and begin implementing the tough but necessary measures that will get their deficits and debt under control.

We hope you have benefited from taking the time to read our lessons, and we also hope that this discussion has prompted some of your own thoughts on other lessons for businesses and for government. Let's hope that economic actors at all levels have learned lessons from this unique episode, and that when the good times return (and they will), we will have taken steps to avoid repeating crucial mistakes. The worst of the recession and financial crisis is over. The need to adapt—in how we act and organize ourselves to avoid the worst impacts of the next financial crisis—is not.

BIBLIOGRAPHY

Alden, Edward. "Protectionism—The Dog That Didn't Bark." *The Globalist*, March 16, 2010.

Baylor, Maximilian, and Louis Beauséjour. "Taxation and Economic Efficiency: Results From a Canadian CGE Model." Federal Department of Finance Working Paper 2004-10. Ottawa: Department of Finance, 2004.

Boards of Trustees of the Federal Hospital Insurance and Federal Supplementary Medical Insurance Trust Funds. *The 2009 Annual Report*. Washington, DC: Boards of Trustees of the Federal Hospital Insurance and Federal Supplementary Medical Insurance Trust Funds, 2009.

Board of Trustees of the Federal Old-Age and Survivors Insurance and Federal Disability Insurance Trust Funds. *The 2009 Annual Report*. Washington, DC: Board of Trustees of the Federal Old-Age and Survivors Insurance and Federal Disability Insurance Trust Funds, 2009.

Bown, Chad P., *Protectionism Continues Its Climb: A Monitoring Update to the Global Antidumping Database*. Washington, DC: World Bank, July 2009.

Colie, Courtney, and Phillip Levine. *Will the Current Economic Crisis Lead to More Retirements?* London: Vox, October 2009.

Congressional Budget Office. *The Long-Term Budget Outlook— June 2010*. Washington, DC: Congressional Budget Office, 2010.

Crawford, Rowena, Carl Emmerson, and Gemma Tetlow. *A Survey of Public Spending in the U.K.* London: Institute for Fiscal Studies, 2009.

Dadayan, Lucy, and Donald J. Boyd. *State Revenue Report*, 77 (October 2009).

de Rugy, Veronique, and Melinda Warren. *Regulatory Agency Spending Reaches New Height: An Analysis of the U.S. Budget for Fiscal Years 2008 and 2009*. St. Louis, MO: Washington University in St. Louis, 2009.

Dixon, Julie. "Too Big to Fail and Embedded Capital." Presentation at the *Financial Services Invitational Forum*. Forum held at Cambridge, Ontario, May 6, 2010.

European Commission. *European Economic Forecast—Spring 2010*. Luxembourg: EC, 2010.

———. *Public Finance in the EMU*. Luxembourg: EC, 2010.

Evenett, Simon J., *Africa Resists the Protectionist Temptation: The 5th GTA Report*. London: Global Trade Alert, May 2010.

Gustman, Alan, Thomas L. Steinmeier, and Nahid Tabatabai. "How Do Pension Changes Affect Retirement Preparedness? The Trend to Defined Contribution Plans and the Vulnerability of the Retirement Age Population to the Stock Market Decline of 2008–09." Presented at the *11th Annual Joint Conference of the Retirement Research Consortium*. Conference held atWashington, DC: August 10–11, 2009.

Hufbauer, Gary Clyde, and Jeffrey J. Schott, *Buy American: Bad for Jobs, Worse for Reputation*. Washington, DC: Peterson Institute for International Economics, February 2009.

International Monetary Fund. *World Economic Outlook—April 2010*. Washington, DC: International Monetary Fund, 2010.

———. "World Economic Outlook Database—April 2010." Washington, DC: IMF, 2010. www.imf.org/external/pubs/ft/weo/2010/01/ weodata/index.aspx (accessed September 7, 2010).

———. *The State of Public Finances Cross-Country Fiscal Monitor: November 3, 2009*. IMF Staff Position Note SPN/09/25. Washington, DC: IMF, 2009.

Kee, Hiau Looi, Cristina Neagu, and Alessandro Nicita. *Is Protectionism on the Rise? Assessing National Trade Policies During the Crisis of 2008*. Policy Research Working Paper. Washington, DC: World Bank, April 2010.

Keynes, John Maynard. *The General Theory of Employment, Interest, and Money*. London: Macmillan, 1936.

Masson, Paul R., and John Pattison. *The Financial Crisis, Regulatory Reform, and International Coordination: What Remains to Be Done*. Ottawa: The Conference Board of Canada, 2010.

———. *International Financial Policy Reform and Options for Canada: Think Globally, Act Locally*. Ottawa: The Conference Board of Canada, 2009.

Population Division of the Department of Economic and Social Affairs of the United Nations Secretariat. *World Population Prospects: The 2008 Revision*. New York: UN, 2009.

Shiller, Robert J. "Animal Spirits Depend on Trust." *The Wall Street Journal*, January 27, 2009.

StatOwl.com. "Operating Systems Market Share." Stat Owl. www.statowl.com/operating_system_market_share.php (accessed September 10, 2010).

Sturgeon, Timothy, and Olga Memedovic. *Looking for Global Value Chains in Trade Statistics: Mapping Structural Change in the World Economy*. Working Paper. Vienna: United Nations Industrial Development Organization, April 14, 2010.

The Conference Board of Canada. *The Determinants of the Retirement Decision*. Unpublished research paper. Ottawa: The Conference Board of Canada, May, 2007.

World Trade Organization. *Report to the TPRB From the Director-General on Trade-Related Developments*. Geneva: WTO, June 14, 2010.

——— *Trade to Expand by 9.5 Per Cent in 2010 After a Dismal 2009, WTO Reports*. News release. Edmonton. Geneva: WTO, March 26, 2010.